D0699992

I'VE BEEN OUT THERE

John and Robin Dickson Series in Texas Music

Sponsored by the Center for Texas Music History
Texas State University–San Marcos
Gary Hartman, General Editor

A list of titles in this series is available at the end of the book.

I'VE BEEN OUT THERE

On the Road with Legends of Rock 'n' Roll

GRADY GAINES WITH ROD EVANS

Texas A&M University Press
College Station

This paper meets the requirements of ANSI/NISO Z39.48-1992
(Permanence of Paper).
Binding materials have been chosen for durability.

Library of Congress Cataloging-in-Publication Data

Gaines, Grady, author.
  I've been out there: on the road with legends of rock 'n' roll / Grady Gaines with
Rod Evans.—First edition.
        pages cm — (John and Robin Dickson series in Texas music)
  Includes bibliographical references and index.
  ISBN 978-1-62349-270-0 (cloth : alk. paper) —
  ISBN 978-1-62349-271-7 (ebook)
  1. Gaines, Grady. 2. Saxophonists—Texas—Biography. 3. Rock musicians—
Texas—Biography. 4. Upsetters (Musical group)—History. 5. Texas Upsetters
(Musical group)—History.NI. Evans, Rod, 1962– author. II. Title.
III. Series: John and Robin Dickson series in Texas music.
  ML419.G235A3   2015
  788.7'166092—dc23
  [B]
                        2014032568

This book is dedicated to my parents, Merkerson Gaines Sr. and Ethel Mae Harris Gaines; my wife, Nell; my entire family; all of my fans; and all of the musicians and performers I've shared a stage with over the years. It's also dedicated to the next generation of musicians and bandleaders who are working to keep their music dreams alive. I hope they benefit from my experience—gained over seven decades and still going strong—as a bandleader.

Special thanks to Susan Criner and Greg Gormanous.

—*Grady Gaines*

I would like to dedicate this book to my mother, Erma Evans, and the memory of my father, Tullie Evans, as well as my family, my lovely wife, Wendy, Roger Sullivan, Taylor and Keleen McNamara, and my sisters, Terri and Kathy Evans.

—*Rod Evans*

Contents

Preface		ix
Acknowledgments		xv
Chapter 1	The Rest Is History	1
Chapter 2	Porch Music	9
Chapter 3	"Cut Out All That Noise!"	18
Chapter 4	Tearing Up Them Houses	22
Chapter 5	Down at Peacock Studios	32
Chapter 6	Like Nothin' They'd Ever Seen	38
Chapter 7	Dancin' and Steppin'	42
Chapter 8	Road Warriors	59
Chapter 9	Exit Stage Left	88
Chapter 10	"Ain't Nothin' for a Stepper"	104
Chapter 11	In the Studio	122
Chapter 12	Still Blowin'	143
Notes		165
Index		167

Preface

From the outside looking in, the itinerant life of the touring musician has a romanticized appeal, especially if you're someone who eschews routine and conformity, but as with any occupation, there are good days and bad days.

Just as professional athletes or actors get to live their lives doing what they love and getting paid for it, professional musicians are afforded an opportunity to make their living playing music—something that comes as natural to them as waking up in the morning. But as many entertainers have discovered, the good fortune of "doing what you love" doesn't come without a price; yet, for many musicians, it's the only life they ever wanted and, despite the pitfalls—fractured families, susceptibility to succumbing to the dark side of the road, loneliness, and financial instability, to name just a few—if given the chance to revisit the start of their career wouldn't change a thing.

I've long been fascinated by the stories of musicians who plied their trade well before the advent of free downloads, YouTube, or Auto-Tune, in the days when radio was the primary source of public exposure and having a hit record still meant something. What we know as the modern recording industry, in which large companies like Columbia and RCA Victor dominated the popular musical landscape, basically coalesced after the Great Depression and experienced its heyday in the 1950s, '60s, and '70s. Musicians of this era generally stood on stage night after night and delivered the goods without the aid of backing tracks, digitally enhanced video presentations, and pyrotechnics. These artists had to move the audience with their instrument, voice, charisma, and stage presence.

However, many of these same performers, especially in the early days, also fell victim to signing recording contracts, through either their own naïveté or the machinations of unscrupulous record company owners looking to cash in on an artist's desperation to secure a record deal. All too frequently that meant that the performer would see very little money from record sales, which made traversing the country playing countless shows the key to success, if not mere survival, in the music business.

As one of the original architects of rock 'n' roll, Little Richard not only developed the blueprint for recording bawdy, sexually suggestive, raucous music that delighted young people and frightened their parents but also set the early standard for living the wild, fast, "rock star" lifestyle, which would become a cliché in the decades after he electrified the music world with his breakout 1955 hit, "Tutti Frutti." If Little Richard's onstage performance and appearance—punctuated by his hyperkinetic movements, banshee singing style, pancake makeup, hair piled three stories high on his head, and out-of-this-world clothes—were over the top, his offstage behavior was certainly just as off the charts.

From 1955 until he shockingly left the music business for the ministry at the height of his powers in 1957, Richard presided over a traveling party that can be modestly described as freewheeling. Alcohol-fueled orgies were a matter of course for Richard and the members of his talented, chick-magnet backing band, the Upsetters. They may not have been the only group of musicians engaging in free love long before the term entered the American consciousness in the 1970s, but they certainly raised fun-loving debauchery to an art form.

Grady Gaines was already a known commodity on Houston's music scene by the time he and fellow Houston sax slinger Clifford Burks accepted an invitation from Richard to join the Upsetters in 1955 just as the star's skyrocket rise to the top of the music charts was beginning. As one of Houston's preeminent sax players and bandleaders, Gaines was well on his way to developing his trademark "honkin'" style of playing before he joined forces with Richard, but signing on with the Upsetters would vault him into the upper echelons of the burgeoning rock 'n' roll, blues, and rhythm and blues scenes, a perch that he would enjoy for nearly two decades.

I first became aware of Grady Gaines in the mid-1990s, when a friend made an off-the-cuff suggestion that I check out an "unbelievable band" playing Sunday nights at Etta's Lounge on Scott Street in Houston's Third Ward. As a result, one Sunday evening I found myself sitting at a small table at Etta's, when my attention was immediately drawn to a burly singer with jet-black processed hair and decked out in a white suit. He was belting out blues with such ferocity and at such a volume that it sounded like his microphone was plugged into a stack of Marshall amplifiers.

I would soon discover two things that night: The three-hundred-plus-pound singer was none other than the late Houston blues belter "Big Robert" Smith, and the unquestioned leader of this impossibly tight band was sax man Grady Gaines. Dressed impeccably in a dark suit with a bright yellow tie, Gaines was wearing glasses that looked like they might have come from the Elton John collection, circa 1975. With its low ceiling, ragged, beer-stained carpet, and small dimensions, the music room at Etta's created a vibe that allowed the grinding, gut-bucket blues and pulsating R&B to penetrate your very soul.

I returned to Etta's a handful of times over the years and never left there feeling anything but uplifted by the sheer power of Grady's sax playing and the talents of his Texas Upsetters band. Grady didn't just stand on stage and blow his saxophone. Trying to restrain Grady by keeping him on that tiny stage would've been like caging a lion fresh off the plains of the Serengeti. He walked through the crowd, stood on top of the rickety tables, and drove the women wild as he gyrated his hips, all the while blowing loud and bold sax solos that sounded like he was playing two instruments at once. This was no-holds-barred musicianship at its best.

I didn't meet Grady on any of those trips to Etta's, although I might have shaken his hand and said something totally unoriginal like "Awesome show, man!" I wouldn't meet him until 2011, after I discovered that he had played with Little Richard in the '50s and a who's who of stars in the '60s. This information prompted me to approach his booking agent, Susan Criner with Gulf Coast Entertainment, to see whether Grady would be open to me pitching an article idea to *Living Blues Magazine* to tell his life story. Grady graciously agreed to be interviewed for the expansive article, which would land on the cover of the August 2011 issue of the publication.

After doing some research on Grady's career to prepare for the article,

I sat down with him several times during the next few weeks. Our one-to-two-hour discussions on his career and life took place in the music room of the beautiful home he shares with his wife, Nell, in the Trinity Gardens neighborhood of northeast Houston. From the very first interview, Grady was gracious and forthright in revealing the good and bad elements of his life, and even though the article was more than three thousand words in length, a sizable amount of information and details still wound up on the cutting-room floor.

When I asked Grady whether he had ever thought of telling his life story in a book, he told me he had been approached by potential authors who had offered to help him put his memoirs together but hadn't met anyone he felt totally comfortable working with. But from the very first time we met, Grady and I seemed to click. Maybe it was because I have a deep respect for him as a musician and a man for what he has accomplished, or maybe it was because I relished hearing tales from the road, or maybe it was because, as a lover of music, especially blues and rock, and an amateur musician myself, I know just enough about playing and performing music to be able to ask questions that music lovers and musicians would ask.

As we dug deeper into the minutiae of his life, it became apparent that some of Grady's recollections of his life had grown fuzzy over the years, which led us to agree to interview friends, family, and current and former band members to help bring color and context to the story. Those contributions proved invaluable in fleshing out the narrative.

One of the first people we contacted was Little Richard, who now lives in Tennessee. Grady and Richard had remained friends over the years, and when we contacted Richard via phone one afternoon, I was pleased to hear that he sounded just as fresh and vital as he always had in TV interviews, with his speech peppered with "honey child" and "Lord, have mercy!" He said he would gladly speak to us about the impact Grady had on the Upsetters and the early part of his career. Unfortunately, as the project proceeded, Richard's health declined steadily, making it difficult to even get in touch with him, and on the rare occasions when he did come to the phone, he was too weak to talk due to a heart attack he suffered in 2013 and a variety of maladies. As a result, the biggest regret that Grady and I share is that we were not able to include any comments from the great Little Richard in this book.

We also regret that there are no comments from Grady's lifelong friend and former bandmate Clifford Burks. Retired and living in New York, Clifford's failing health prevented him from participating in the project. He passed away in October 2014 at age 84.

Thanks to Grady's diligence and willingness to reveal himself, as well as the candid recollections of friends, family, and musical collaborators who shared many of the same experiences, we feel we have fashioned a book that faithfully tells the story of a man who played a crucial role in the birth of rock 'n' roll and whose bold, in-your-face style of sax playing influenced countless others who would follow him on the road and in the studio. It's the story of a dedicated sideman turned bandleader who did whatever it took to help the artists he was backing sound their best, while also captivating audiences with his talent, attention to detail, athleticism, and boundless energy.

In 2014, Grady was recognized for his pioneering role in the development of rock 'n' roll, blues, and rhythm and blues when he headlined the second class of inductees into the *Houston Press* Houston Music Hall of Fame. While the honor paid tribute to a career spanning over 60 years, Grady, who continues to perform as the leader of Grady Gaines and the Texas Upsetters, remains an immensely popular entertainer.

It has truly been an honor for me to get to know Grady and Nell and to work with them both to help tell his story, and we hope you enjoy this honest look at the life of a man who has "been out there" for seven decades.

—Rod Evans

Acknowledgments

Many people graciously gave of their time and expertise to assist us over the course of the nearly three years it took to produce this book. We would like to offer our heartfelt thanks to all.

Roger Wood, the author of the excellent book *Down in Houston: Bayou City Blues* (with photographer James Fraher) and a former professor at Houston Community College, provided invaluable assistance with the preparation of the proposal that would eventually lead to the publication of this book and provided sound advice throughout the process. Grady's booking agent, Susan Criner, president of Gulf Coast Entertainment, offered crucial support throughout the project.

Many of Grady's friends, family members, and current and former bandmates agreed to be interviewed for the book, and their recollections of events and insights into Grady, the original Upsetters, the Texas Upsetters, and the music industry in general lent crucial detail and context. We thank them all for their time and energy. They include Grady's family: Nell Pharms, Adrena Carter, Roy Gaines, L. C. Gaines, Reba Jones, Grady Gaines Jr., Elmore Harris, and Wilkie Hartwell.

Grady's longtime friends, associates, and former and current band members who assisted us are Milton Hopkins, Greg Gormanous, Hammond Scott, Patrick Harris, Charles "Chuck" Connor, Earlie Huntsberry Lewis, Paul David Roberts, Reginald Yarborough, Nelson Mills III, Robert Lewis, Bill Sadler, Coby Emery, Etta Emery, and John Andrews. A big thank-you goes out to Tom McLendon, owner of the Big Easy Social and Pleasure Club, one of Houston's premier blues nightspots and a frequent venue for Grady Gaines and the Texas Upsetters, for his long-term support of local blues and musicians.

Other contributors include transcriptionist Anne Arnold, and attorney Terri Evans. Thanks to the entire staff at Texas A&M University Press, especially Thom Lemmons, Katie Duelm, Holli Koster, Kyle Littlefield, David Neel, and Kathryn M. Krol.

—Rod Evans

I'VE BEEN OUT THERE

The Rest Is History

I was in Houston with my first band, the Blues Ramblers, when "Tutti Frutti" became a major hit, and Little Richard called and said he wanted me to meet him in Brandywine, Maryland, outside of Washington, DC, in about a week. He actually wanted me to bring (Blues Ramblers bandmate and saxophonist) Clifford (Burks) with me, but we had to make up our minds real quick because the Ramblers were going great. I mean, we was playing four hours a night, seven nights a week. You could almost say we were playing eight nights a week because on maybe three of those nights after we finished our main gig, we'd go to another club and play after hours for about four more hours.

But we thought about it for a couple of days and decided we'd join him, so he sent two airplane tickets, one for me and one for Clifford, and we met him in Brandywine. The rest was history. We was on tour constantly, and the only time we stopped was when Richard quit to be a preacher.

Me and Clifford played a lot of dates with Richard before he left Houston (where he performed frequently with a popular group called the Tempo Toppers) to go solo, so we got real familiar with his music, which helped out when he asked us to join his band. We played all around Houston and some other towns with Richard before he had us come to Brandywine. That's why we knew his music like we did.

As we went along, we picked up different people in the band, but when we joined Richard in 1955, he already had the name the Upsetters for his band. We had Thomas Hartwell on guitar, and we had Wilbur Smith, who later on changed his name to Lee Diamond, from New Orleans, playing keyboards and saxophone. We had Sammy Parker on sax from Richmond, Virginia, and Charles Connor from New Orleans was the drummer, and on baritone sax we had this kid from New Orleans, Shake Snyder. Later on, Larry Lanier joined up on baritone sax, and we had O. C. Robertson, "Bassie," from Richmond, Virginia, on bass. So we had five sax players, including three tenor players. At one time, we had five tenors. Richard loved them tenor saxes, and he worked 'em real hard, too!

Charles "Chuck" Connor, Upsetters' drummer

RICHARD SAID, "I know two good-looking guys from Houston, Texas, named Grady Gaines and Clifford Burks, and I've sent for them to join the band." Richard had just bought a Mercury station wagon that pulled a trailer that read "Mr. Tutti Frutti: Little Richard's Upsetters" on the side that we used to get to gigs. That's what we picked Grady and Clifford up in from the airport. The first time I saw Grady, I thought he's a good-looking guy who probably got a lot of girls. He could play his instrument and made the band sound good. We were used to playing with Richard with just a couple horns, so we were excited to get those guys. Grady turned out to be the bandleader and musical director, and since they (Gaines and Burks) were both from Texas and I was from Louisiana (New Orleans), I was familiar with that sound. I think the first gig we played with them was at an armory, and it was a big crowd. Grady looked good out there on the bandstand, and having him and Clifford changed the whole dynamic of the band because we had two tenor saxes now. Lee Diamond played alto and tenor sax (in addition to piano), and it made the band sound more powerful.

When we first saw Richard, he looked pretty much the same as the last time we saw him in Houston. He always wore that makeup, and he had that same curly hair that looked like a lady would have her hair fixed back in that day, but it looked real good. He wore that pancake makeup, number 29, I think it was called. He called himself the "Georgia Peach," and he looked good enough to be a peach. His skin would be so pretty and had such a beautiful color to it.

We played a gig the night we got to town, only a couple of hours after

The Upsetters on tour with Little Richard, circa 1955. From top left, Nathaniel Douglas, Charles Connor, O. C. "Bassie" Robertson, Lee Diamond, Clifford Burks, Little Richard, Grady. Photo from the Grady Gaines Collection.

Grady (in hat) and O. C. "Bassie" Robertson on tour with Little Richard, around 1956. Photo courtesy of the Milton Hopkins Collection.

we got there. On that first gig, I think we were wearing Bermuda shorts because it was the summertime, and it was burning up hot, so we just put a shirt and shorts on and went out and played through the night. Richard was electric up there, and the crowd just went wild the whole night! At the beginning, we did a lot of traveling in the station wagon pulling a trailer. We had two station wagons sometimes. Eventually we got a GMC truck and made it into what a van is today: extended it, put more seats in it, a luggage rack on the top. We didn't have to pull no trailer once we got that going, and we used that for a long time. We traveled in buses when we went on shows that had maybe ten to fifteen other acts, but we didn't have a (private charter) bus like they do nowadays. It just was different then. We was at the top of the totem pole and had everything first class, but it just wasn't like it is now.

We didn't have no days off after we joined up with the Upsetters; we probably played thirty-three straight days or more. At the time, Richard was hot, hot, so everybody (promoters) that could get him would try to get him on as many dates as they could. We played the East Coast first, then we started heading south to Washington, DC, Richmond, Roanoke, the Carolinas, Georgia. Anywhere a promoter could get a date on Richard we would play in those towns because everyone knew they would make money.

We played all through the South, through Alabama, Louisiana, up through Texas and then out west to Arizona, California, and up the West Coast to Portland and Vancouver, Canada. We just didn't stop, but we was young and could handle it, plus we was having fun doing it. In those days there wasn't no flying to the gigs, although Richard would fly sometimes, but the band traveled in the station wagons, and we just put all of our equipment and uniforms and stuff in the trailer and headed on down the road. You'd make sure you left in plenty of time so you could take your time and enjoy it. It wasn't no life that we didn't enjoy even though there was a lot of prejudices out there, but other than that, we enjoyed it, and that's what made it so good. All of the band members got along real well from the start, and we had a lot of fun. Plus, Richard was super to work for. If you needed anything, he'd help you.

Because "Tutti Frutti" was a big hit, everywhere we'd play was jam-packed, and we didn't play exactly like the record on stage; we always added to it, gave it more lift. Whatever Richard did, we followed him wherever he'd carry us to in a song. We'd be going there with him and be dancin' and steppin'. We didn't just stand there and play. We were moving around, walking through the audience. We'd do a little of everything, then I'd be up on top of the piano. Man, it was *something*.

We didn't rehearse any of our steps; we just did them on stage. If one man in the front line started doing a step, the rest of us would join in, or if I started it, the rest would join in with what I was doing. It was follow-the-leader. We didn't rehearse 'em like people do today; we just did it automatically. We did anything to move the crowd, and when they started liking it, we kept on doing it until we had steps for just about every number.

The crowds would go crazy, and a lot of 'em (female fans) were fainting. Some shows you'd see 'em carrying three or four of 'em out; they just had no control. Little Richard was just magic to 'em, and then his band was magic itself because he had all nice-looking guyls in there. We were all playing the part and had plenty of spirit, so it was a good team. Everywhere we'd play, if a band was working in town, they'd try to take off and be in that front row to see what we were doing. After the show, they'd be asking us questions like "What kind of mouthpiece you using?" or "How do you do this or that?" Some would have little tape recorders with 'em.

Richard did everything spontaneous on stage, and whatever he did, we'd just follow him, and when you do that every night for so long, it's not hard because it comes natural. Richard might do an hour show sometimes, but it depended on how he felt. But he worked real hard. He was a hardworking guy.

You can't hardly imagine how famous Richard got. He got so famous that it was kind of a problem for him sometimes. I mean, women was trying to tear his clothes off at every show. But he had enough security around him to keep people from getting to him (offstage). Couldn't nobody get to him unless he wanted them to. But even early on when he was *hot, hot, hot,* Richard started dropping hints that he was gonna leave music and be a preacher, but we never took that serious until years later when he finally did it.

The crowds we played for were mostly white, but me and Clifford knew what we were going into. In Houston with the Blues Ramblers, we played in front of whites and blacks, but it was mostly black. But it didn't matter to me and Clifford one way or another. We were ready and got out there and did what we needed to do.

But in my experience anyway, black and white crowds are a little different. With the black crowd, it all depended on if you played what they wanted to hear. If you played what they wanted to hear, you got a hell of a feedback from them, but with the white crowd, if you play what they want to hear, then play some things that are not so big in the crossover with them, they still showed a whole lot more appreciation than if it was vice versa. With the black crowd, if you play something they don't particularly like, then they gonna let you know by not giving you the kind of response you're looking for.

By this time, people like Pat Boone was doing covers of Little Richard's tunes ("Tutti Frutti" and "Long Tall Sally"), and that didn't really bother me. I thought it was good that he did it and would be good for Richard. Richard didn't like it at the time, but later on I think he realized it was a help to him because it helped broaden his repertoire for selling records. I thought Pat Boone singing "Tutti Frutti" wasn't nothing like Little Richard singing it. It sounded more like somebody talking it. When you heard Richard sing it, you could hear that big difference. But Pat Boone had his way of doing it, and it sold records, and that's all that matters. Elvis sang some of Richard's songs, too ("Tutti Frutti," "Long Tall Sally," "Rip It Up," "Ready Teddy"), and I thought he could get away with it better than Pat Boone because Elvis had the kind of voice that was closer to Richard's, and he had a lot of showmanship.

Early on, Richard had the idea to make the band dress and look like we was gay so it wouldn't upset the whites who thought that we might be after their women! You know, people have their ideas about you, and when we went through the different theaters playing one-nighters, at a lot of places people would say we were all gay. What people fix in their mind is what they think it is, so they didn't worry about you because they thought you were gay, so they think you ain't gonna fool around with their women. It kind of eased that way of thinking and made them more comfortable if they thought we were gay and wouldn't have no problems out of us, but the girls were still after us big time.

Grady, Little Richard, and O. C. "Bassie" Robertson on stage at the Apollo Theater, New York, circa 1956. Photo from the Grady Gaines Collection.

The Upsetters had women in every city, town, village, you name it. Our reputation for women was at the highest, and they went crazy for us wherever we went. I remember one time we played in Jacksonville (Florida), and we heard that even though the rumor was that we was gay, when husbands knew we were coming to town, they would try to keep their wives at home, but we'd still have women there anyway. We heard husbands started being real nice to their wives when we were coming to town, too.

I remember we were playing at a festival in Virginia one night, near Chesapeake Bay, and one of the promoters was black. Me and his fine, young daughter took to each other, and the dressing rooms had beds in them, so I got her in there and started grinding on that meat, but the girl's father was trying to find his daughter and was walking around with a sawed-off, double-barrel shotgun. He was going from room to room knocking on doors, and when he knocked on the room we was in, I heard Clifford say, "They ain't in there. I saw 'em over there somewhere," and he went on down the hall. If he had opened that door and caught us in there, he would have wiped me out.

Porch Music

What inspired me and my brother, Roy, to get into the music world was my grandfather, Andy Gaines. He was a violin player, and he used to play on the buses going from town to town, making tips. He played the harmonica, too. My daddy played harmonica real well, too, and helped to start the musical roots in me and Roy.

My daddy, Merkerson Gaines, played harmonica mostly on the porch of our house in Waskom, Texas, where I was born on May 14, 1934. He played stuff like Lead Belly and those kinds of cats. It was mostly blues and whatever was happening back in that time. Our house was actually about five miles outside of Waskom and up on a little hill. I remember the house was one of them shotgun houses, with one big room and two little rooms. There was nine people living in the house, including seven kids and my mama and daddy. We didn't have no electricity, and we had to use an outhouse. There was one fireplace for the wintertime, and, boy, it got real hot in the summertime. The seven kids were Reba, the oldest, followed by Merkerson Jr., L. C., Adrena, and then came me, followed by Roy and our baby sister, Wilkie.

Waskom was a real small town. Back then maybe five thousand people lived there. We lived on a farm and killed hogs and had a smokehouse, where we kept ham and beef and sausage. Oh yeah, we had plenty of good meat all the time, it seems. On an average day if we wasn't in school, we got up early in the morning to feed the cows, hogs, and chickens, then we'd go down to the fields—corn, cotton, peanuts—we grew everything. It was hard work, and you'd be glad to get home and eat. Pretty much everything we had food-wise we raised, but we bought a few things from the store in town, like flour, meal, sugar, cold cuts, and stuff like that.

L. C. Gaines, Grady's older brother

THERE WASN'T NOTHING GOING ON in Waskom. All we did was gin cotton and work on the farm. We raised some cows and hogs and chickens, and I remember we had one horse. We might go into town maybe two or three times a week. We walked them five miles to and from school every day, too. I think our closest neighbor was about a mile away on each side of us, and if we wanted to go see a movie or something, we usually went over to Shreveport, where some of our mama's brothers and sisters lived, which was about twenty miles away.

We used to fry up fatback all the time, and, man, was it good. I remember it would usually be a cold day when we had to slaughter them hogs, and we did it together as a family. You had to hit the hog in the head or get him in the throat with a knife. Whatever they decided to kill that day, whether it was a hog or a chicken, we did it together, and we would eat off that until the next year. Where we lived, in the black area of town, there was just a gas station and a little store. The white folks mainly lived in town.

We didn't have a whole lot of race problems in Waskom because it wasn't like some of them other Jim Crow towns where you had hangings and stuff going on. Basically, if you behaved yourself, you got along OK.

L. C. Gaines

OUR GRANDMOTHER WAS PRETTY ROUGH on those white folks; she would talk back to 'em. So we didn't have much trouble because everybody knew our grandmother and grandfather. We had a cousin, B. Flanagan, that got killed, though. A man named J. P. Jones shot him because he had supposedly stolen a cow, but you know he wasn't going to steal no cow. Anyway, B. walked away from him, and when the man said, "Wait. Turn around," he didn't turn around, so the man shot him in the back. We had another cousin who got hung on a fence. I can't remember his

Grady's parents, Merkerson Gaines Sr. and Ethel Mae Harris Gaines. Photo from the Grady Gaines Collection.

name or what caused it, but one weekend they hung him on that fence along Highway 80 right out of Greenwood (Louisiana).

Our mama, Ethel Mae Harris Gaines, came from Bethany, Louisiana. She was a real good woman, a little woman and one of the best people around. Later, after we moved to Houston, we lived on Atwater Street across from the Sunshine Missionary Baptist Church, and that church depended on her a whole lot. She was a churchgoing woman and raised all seven of us that way. She had a little help from Daddy, but she was the basis of making sure every last one of us worked. Once we moved to Houston, we had to work and give her some money every week. It was her way of showing us the way and what you were going to have to confront in your life as time passed. If you didn't come up with that money, you had some trouble out of her.

I never didn't come up with the money, but I remember one time when we lived in Houston, and I got a little sassy, so she threw my clothes and stuff under a big tree. I stayed with my girlfriend and her mother for a while. I'm stubborn, and my mama was stubborn, so I didn't call, and she didn't call, but she finally came and got me. But she did things to make you grow up and be a real person and man. I learned a lot of lessons from that lady, and I use a lot of them now. That's what gets me through this world today—going back and picking up on things she taught us.

Our daddy was from East Texas and was about my height (about six feet tall) and a handsome man. The women were crazy about him, like they were with me, so I guess I took some of that after him. He worked in a lumberyard mainly, but he had some side hustles, too, because he had all these kids and had to help take care of 'em. He started making a little moonshine, and I'll never forget when Merk (Merkerson Jr.) and L. C. drank some of that whiskey.

L. C. Gaines

HE HAD THE WHISKEY in five-gallon jugs, and we would take about half a pint out, pour water in it, and mix it up with sugar. Well, the customers started complaining, but he didn't know what happened until our sister Adrena told on us. He thought we had ruined his whiskey, so he whipped the both of us. The old man would whip you for thirty minutes straight sometimes.

If daddy told you to do something, and you didn't do it, he got into that rump with whatever he could get his hands on—a switch, a belt, an electric cord. But I didn't get no whippings, though, that I remember because I was mostly quiet and obeyed because I didn't want none of that. But when he whipped (my sisters and brothers), he'd whip 'em, then talk for a while—"I told you not to do that"—then whip 'em again. He'd whip you until he got tired. But it wasn't mean. Usually it was for not doing what he told them to do catching up with 'em after he had told 'em so many times. He did that to show us not to do that no more. I think they ought to do more of that today, and people wouldn't be the way they are. Kids

The Houston home on Atwater Street, where Grady and his family lived when Grady was about twelve years old. Photo by Rod Evans.

would obey their parents. I appreciate my parents for it, and I appreciate every second of how they raised us.

We didn't do much for fun in Waskom. About all we did was go swimming in this little pond or go fishing. We spent a lot of time cutting wood for the winter. About the biggest thing we had was called Fourth Sunday. That was in August, and it was *the* big day in the country. Everybody from all around would bring food in wagons and meet at the church. You could go to anybody's wagon and eat whatever you wanted. They be done killed hogs, cows, chickens—whatever you wanted—and all the country people would get together. It was like a holiday, and it would be one heck of a day. People from down there still talk about it.

When Daddy left Waskom to work at a lumberyard in Houston, Mama, Daddy, and Merkerson Jr. went to Houston first, and the rest of us stayed in Waskom. We also spent some time in Louisiana with some

Roy Gaines, Merkerson Gaines Jr., Elmore Harris, Grady, and L. C. Gaines in the early '90s. Photo from the Grady Gaines Collection.

aunts until Mama and Daddy got everything established in Houston. It was less than a year, I think, before we all moved to Houston.

I must have been around eight or nine years old when we moved into the first house in Houston at 2216 Lucas Street in the Fifth Ward. It was a brand-new house in a brand-new neighborhood. It had two bedrooms, and it was real nice for that time. I remember there being lots of houses on the street and an ice cream parlor and Ted's Filling Station down the street. It was mostly black people and Mexicans living there at the time.

It was about that time that Uncle Elmore Harris, my mama's brother, moved in with us for a while. He was the baby brother out of thirteen kids, and he was more like a brother to us. He was around the family all the time and was there for us through a big part of our life. We kind of patterned ourselves after him because he was out there first, making money by driving taxis for the Crystal White Cab Company, which was the cab company for black folks back then in Houston. He eventually got Merk Jr. driving cabs, too, and eventually owned around thirty-five cabs. I think the whole town owes him a lot because he helped build the town as far as getting black people where they needed to go. All of the brothers looked up to him and still do.

Elmore Harris, Grady's uncle

THE FIRST THING I WAS TOLD after I finished school—because
I couldn't find a job—was to go to Houston. I had a '36 Ford that
I drove there and went to the waterfront (Houston Ship Channel
area), where I had a friend that drove a cab. He told me, "I want
you to drive for me Saturday and Sunday." I said OK. That first
Saturday, I made $23. On Sunday I made $25. I had just gotten
a job at Hughes Tool Company, and I asked the boss for a leave.
He told me he couldn't give me a leave because I was too good of
a worker, but I said I'm going anyway, so I put my car on the taxi
line. That was big money in those days. Then I took my car and
put it on the line with the Crystal White Cab Company. First, I
got up to four cars, then I wound up with thirty-five taxis. I made
some good money.

I was watching Uncle Elmore because he was doing what I wanted to
do: make some money. I remember one time Uncle Elmore bought
ten cabs at one time with $300,000. How could you not want to fol-
low someone like that? I never did drive a cab, but I knew I had to
do something because I saw him getting all those pretty women! He
was my idol because he was the top man, and he did it right. To this
day, Roy won't go nowhere without a suit and tie, and that comes from
Uncle Elmore. Same with me. If I'm going on a business meeting or
something, I'm gonna be dressed. Every one of us brothers were like
that because he set such a powerful example for us on how to express
yourself. He also was part of the reason why I put so much into our
clothes and looking good on stage when I started playing music.

   After we lived on Lucas Street for about three years, we moved to a
house on Noble Street, which wasn't far from our old house. We probably
lived there about three years, too. Right after we moved there was when
me and Roy started a paper route for the *Houston Chronicle.*

Roy Gaines, Grady's younger brother

I RECALL there was some railroad tracks running right by our house, and those tracks were pretty dangerous. A couple of people got hurt on them, and I remember a guy named Charlie, a dark-skinned guy who lived a couple of streets over from us. He was trying to cross those tracks one morning and got killed. There was another time when me and Grady went crawfishing with some boys at this crawfish hole across the tracks. We got over there and our little sister, Wilkie, had followed us, so Grady, being the oldest there, told me to take her back home because she didn't have no business being there. But my contention was that I didn't want to take her home because I was there to catch some crawfish, and there wouldn't be any left when I got back. But in our family, whoever was oldest was in charge, so I had to heed what Grady said and take her back. After I took her home, I was in such a hurry to get back to the crawfish hole, and there was two trains coming: one going south and one north. The one going north was closest to me and was backing up, and I needed to get across the tracks. I knew I could beat the train farthest away from me, but with all the noise from both trains, I ran into the caboose of the train backing up and cracked my skull. I was in the hospital for about a month, but I was eventually OK.

We threw the paper route on our bicycles that had those racks on either side of the back wheel, and you'd ride down the street flingin' 'em into people's yards. I wound up being what they called the station captain and was in charge of about fifty-seven routes, which pretty much covered the whole Fifth Ward. Being the station captain meant if somebody decided to quit their route, I would have to throw it until I found somebody else to do it, and sometimes two or three people would quit at the same time. But we made about thirty-five cents a week from each customer throwing them papers. By this time, we were going to E. O. Smith Junior High, and I wore a suit and tie every day to school from the money we made on the paper route. I was the sharpest student in school.

Me and Roy really wanted to buy a saxophone with the money from the paper route. I remember Mama and I rode together to Parker Music Company and she cosigned for me to get it, but I had to pay for it. That first sax was just a plain King tenor; they didn't have the (King) Super 20s yet. As soon as I got it home, I started trying to play it. I had some books that showed you how to hold the whole notes and finger them.

Roy Gaines

I WANTED TO PLAY the saxophone myself at first, but I found out since I got hit by that train, I couldn't play a wind instrument, so Mama helped me buy a piano, which stayed in the family for a long time.

My oldest brother, Merkerson, bought the piano from the family, and he still owned it when he passed away at eighty-five years old in October of 2012.

CHAPTER 3

"Cut Out All That Noise!"

I wanted to play the sax like Louis Jordan, who was *hot, hot, hot* at the time. He was the one that mostly inspired me to play, but there were others like Gene Ammons, Arnett Cobb, and Illinois Jacquet that I looked up to. I remember our neighbor, a guy named R. P. (Roger Paul) Wallace, who used to play saxophone, and I would hear him from our house. He played some Louis Jordan, but he played some jazz and some sweet songs like "Stardust" and "Body and Soul," too. He could play anything. He was a short guy, maybe a little over five feet tall, and probably in his late twenties then, and he always stayed sharp. He had this gig bag that he put his saxophones in, and I used to see him walking to his gigs on the weekends. I'd be sitting on the porch, and he would be steppin' and lookin' clean, and I wanted to be like that.

Louis Jordan was one of the most influential musicians of the 1930s, '40s, and '50s. His hyperkinetic performing style helped usher in the arrival of R&B and eventually rock 'n' roll. Buoyed by his superb backing band, the Tympany Five, Jordan was a virtuoso on the alto sax and infused his seemingly endless stream of hits with an infectious energy and sense of humor. Born in Arkansas in 1908, Jordan was a hit-making machine for Decca Records, beginning in the late '30s. He hit his stride during the World War II years, when he recorded extensively for the Armed Forces Radio Service. Hits like "G. I. Jive," "Caldonia," "Choo Choo Ch'Boogie," "Saturday Night Fish Fry," and many others made Jordan one of the earliest black performers to rack up big sales figures in pop music.

Listen to any of Jordan's catalog, and you'll see how his expressive, boogie-soaked, rough-edged playing style informed Grady Gaines's own "honkin'" delivery. Thanks to the trove of short films and "soundies" that he left behind, it's also apparent that Jordan's onstage antics, rambunctious wordplay, and dedication to showmanship played a huge role in Grady's development as a performer. Jordan died in 1975 at the age of sixty-seven.[1]

Me and Roy started taking lessons from Mrs. Punch, who lived across the railroad tracks from us. She was a nice-looking lady, kind of tall; put me in the mind of Della Reese. We took lessons at the same time, and Roy started out on the sax but switched to piano, then later the guitar. I think we paid fifty or seventy-five cents for an hour lesson. I took lessons from Mrs. Punch until I got into junior high school, where Mr. (George) McGruder was the band teacher. I played in the marching band and the orchestra. I remember it was a big deal when I first played "Caldonia," at least it was to me. Then Jimmy Forrest came out with "Night Train," and I learned how to play that real good, and people started requesting I play it over and over again.

Roy Gaines

WE LIVED close to a team of brothers named Clarence and Sweets Holliman, and they were a bit more advanced than we were in the music thing. They were playing in clubs at an early age, and Sweets was a duplicate of (pianist) Charles Brown. He could sing and play the piano just like Brown could, and I think he taught Clarence how to play with him on guitar just like the guitar players that played with Charles Brown at the time. Clarence had a real distinct style, kind of close to (blues guitarist) Johnny Moore. He had a special way of playing the blues. At that time, Charles Brown was bigger than life to us. He had some songs out that were big hits for us in Houston, including "Black Night" and "Driftin' Blues." Clarence could play those songs with his brother singing on piano, and that put them a step ahead of Grady and I, but they really got us even more interested in music.

Calvin Owens was a student teacher at school, and he taught me a lot about playing and how to handle myself as a musician. He taught me how to hold the mouthpiece and how to count out so many beats. I started off counting four beats and holding that tone throughout, then I'd move up to eight beats for two measures and then on up to twelve beats for three measures and up to sixteen beats. Holding those notes as long as you could helped you get your embouchure and develop your sound. He was the first one to show me how to do that. Of course, as I went through my career I ran across all types of people that I learned stuff from, but he was the first.

Calvin Owens, who died in 2008 at age seventy-eight, was a legendary Houston trumpeter and bandleader. He's probably best known for serving two stints as the bandleader with B. B. King and for his work as a session player at Houston's Peacock Studios in the 1950s. He was a major contributor to King's 1983 Grammy Award–winning album, *Blues 'n' Jazz*."[2]

I started practicing three, four hours a day. I would come home from school, throw papers, then start practicing. I didn't have a lot else to do, and I really wanted to learn how to play it. My practicing would bug the neighbors sometimes. I'd hear 'em hollering, "Grady, cut out all that noise you making over there! You ain't gonna ever do nothing." Well, I guess I made a liar out of 'em.

L. C. Gaines

GRADY AND ROY kept us awake all night, with Grady practicing his horn and Roy playing on the piano until he switched to

guitar. But I could see that they had talent because that's all they
did. They never had no jobs other than throwing papers.

I did OK in school, and we played a lot of football in the schoolyard and
sometimes in the vacant lots. They said I could run that ball real good,
but I didn't play on the school team. Shit, I wasn't gonna let them boys
be hittin' my ass! I was probably a C-plus or B student, but, of course, my
favorite subjects were music and girls. I remember one time I told Mama
I was gonna quit school and get a job, but the first job I had was unload-
ing train boxcars filled with lumber. I worked part of one day and left. I
thought, "I don't want to deal with this!" That was a hard job, and it let
me know I wanted to play the horn.

By junior high I already had some girls, and I think I lost my virginity
when I was about twelve or thirteen. Probably the first girl I was with was
Evelyn Wright, but we were just sort of hittin' it. I had my first girlfriend
about this time: Faye Shotwell. She was the first girl I really cared about,
and she would become Grady Jr.'s (and Debra's) mama later on. But I
always got attention from girls, going all the way back to elementary
school, where I had girls bringing me money and donuts and whatever I
wanted.

That kind of thing followed me through life. I couldn't help it because
I was pretty! But God made me. I didn't. Thanks to my mother and
father and no plastic surgery, I was just plain ol' pretty.

In junior high, there were these two girls, Joanne Reed and Joanne
Chambers, that kept my name hot by sending in requests to radio sta-
tions. In those days you would write on postcards and send them in asking the DJ "Will you play such and such song for Grady Gaines?" They
did that so much that it got other girls to start writing in, and it got so
popular until the DJs would announce on the air, "Whoever this Grady
Gaines is, I want to see who you are, so come on down to the station."

I would go down there, and they would say, "I see why now" because
I stayed sharp. I was gonna get some of that attention. That whole thing
lasted through school until I dropped out in the tenth grade. That goes
back to Uncle Elmore. I wanted to follow his style of life.

CHAPTER 4

"Tearing Up Them Houses"

By the time I was in high school, I was playing a lot of little gigs and was definitely thinking that I wanted a life in music because I wanted to get out there and make some of that money that Louis Jordan was making. I used to go see him when he'd come to Houston to play at the City Auditorium. It seemed like he came to town every Labor Day. I wanted that to be my life. That time was what I call the "honkin' time." You could take one note, and if you knew how to use it, you could do a whole lot with it.

I went to Wheatley High School, where Sammy Harris was the band teacher. He was a real good teacher, and a bunch of people like my brother Roy, Clarence Holliman, and (guitarist) Milton Hopkins were all in the same school and in the band program. Hubert Laws and the Jazz Crusaders and Joe Sample came behind my class. One day at Wheatley, Illinois Jacquet came through and played at an assembly. It was one of the real good memories of my beginning music. He was real exciting and inspired me because he had some hip records out, like "Flying Home." It was right after that assembly that I started feeling like I could make a living at music.

I was about fourteen or fifteen when I formed my first band, Grady Gaines and His House Rockers. Then I joined the Harlem Music Makers, which was led by Oddis Turner. After that, I started the Blues Ramblers. Oddis and Milton Hopkins was in the Harlem Music Makers, but after they left that group, we became the Blues Ramblers. Oddis played keyboards and sang, and he went on to become a professor at Texas Southern University but passed away a few years back. He was a real lover of Fats Domino, and Little Richard would tell you that he got some of his style from Oddis. I had Floyd Arceneaux, who was very

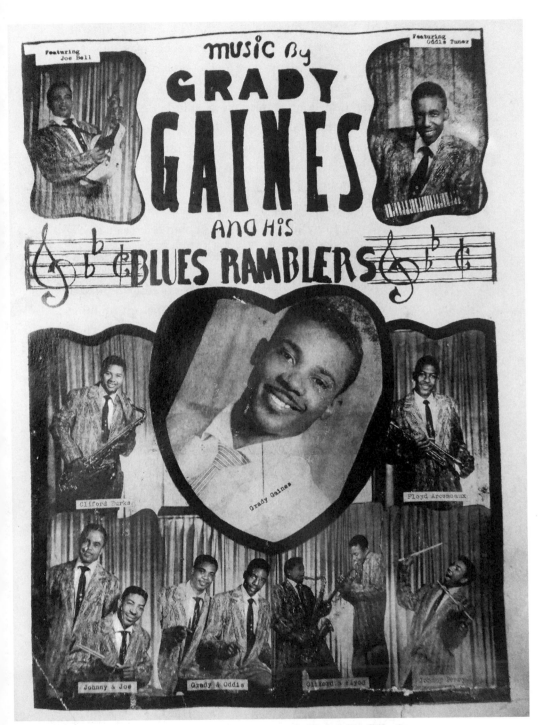

Early Blues Ramblers promotional poster. Photo from the Grady Gaines Collection.

well known and educated, playing trumpet. I had Joe Bell on guitar and vocals, and he could play anything T-Bone Walker could play. I had Clifford Burks on saxophone and Johnny Perry, who wound up playing with me for about thirty years, on drums.

Couldn't nobody beat Johnny playing a shuffle. All of T-Bone Walker's stuff was a shuffle, and we played a lot of T-Bone. Even right now, Johnny could play a shuffle if you wanted a shuffle. You had to play it a certain way with the cymbals and the bass (kick) drum, and you could feel it, too, when he played that shuffle.

After me and Clifford left to join Little Richard on the road, some of the Ramblers went into the army. Oddis was going to college anyway. Johnny Perry went with Chuck Willis' band. Joe Bell was real popular in Houston and wound up leading his own band.

We played at the nightclubs and also at a lot of social clubs, like the Rainbow Social Club and the Creole Knights, and some private things. We played mostly cover songs, but we had some original stuff, too. At the Club Matinee this DJ named King Bee (Clifton Smith) would broadcast his show from a studio in the back that had these big glass windows. Man, he was *hot, hot, hot* then, and those shows really helped us to get out there. Roy started out playing piano with us sometimes, and I'll tell you what, we was tearing up them houses!

Roy Gaines

I WAS PLAYING PIANO with Grady's band, but the first time I saw Grady going around the club blowing his horn and all the girls following him back to the stage, that's when I decided I didn't want to play piano because I couldn't walk around and get the girls. That got me to playing the guitar. I took lessons from a white guy named Steve Hairston, who was a great player. I got his name out of the newspaper. He hooked me up and taught guitar the same way Mrs. Punch used to teach us music. He taught me three or four songs that were real popular, like T-Bone Walker's "Cold, Cold Feeling" and Gatemouth Brown's "Boogie Woogie Rambler." Everybody thought I was a fourteen-year-old sensation, so that's what they started calling me.

We started playing a lot at the Club Matinee over on Lyons Avenue. They would have bands play in a room called the Anchor Room, which is where most of the shows was held. The Club Matinee was like a restaurant, but they would have bands in the Anchor Room. They brought in all the name people like Bobby ("Blue") Bland, Charles Brown, Sonny Thomas, Lonnie Johnson, Lionel Hampton, and Amos Wilburn. It was a compact deal for everybody that would come through, at least the black stars, and later some white acts would come through because they had a hotel, liquor store, and barbershop all right together, so everybody that came to town would stay at the Crystal White Hotel. A lot of 'em would be here so often that it was like home for them. People like Bobby Bland would come here so often that he eventually got himself an apartment.

The Club Matinee was the most modern place around, and, man, it was fabulous. It was owned by a guy named Mr. Dixon, who was half white, I think. There was a movie theater (the DeLuxe) across the street, and the Crystal White Cab Company, where my uncle Elmore drove a cab, was next door.

But the band really got popular when we started playing at a place called Whispering Pines. It became our main club, and we were the house band there for a while. Whispering Pines was owned by Joe Oakman, who owned Oakman Cleaners on Jensen Drive. We stayed busy. We worked five, six, seven nights a week, and we made OK money. Of course, back then you could do a lot more with a little money. It went like this: You had your five-cent gigs, but a $5 gig was a fair gig (each member got $5). If you made $7, $8, or $10 in a night, that was about tops and a pretty good gig.

The bandleader might make $20 a night, and I was the bandleader. But as the leader, you had more responsibilities, and everything falls on you. When it all boiled down, you were almost better off being back with the sidemen. I did a lot of things as the bandleader that made no money, and my mama would say, "Grady, I wouldn't do that." But I said, "Mama, this is what I want to do."

They had a floor show with dancers and a comic act called Mike and Ace. They were a brother and sister act, and they were really good. There was another comic team named Vootie and Wootie, and they were a hell of a team that would dance and clown and get the crowd all excited. The crowds was mostly Negroes and Spanish people, but some whites came, too, every now and then, and it was jam-packed every weekend.

Mr. Oakman would bring in people like Clifton Chenier, who would play that zydeco, and there would be cars lined up as far as you can see. He would bring in people that had maybe one or two hit records out, like Amos Wilburn, Big Joe Turner, T-Bone Walker, Nappy Brown, Smiley Lewis, and many more. They'd be playing in town, and he'd grab them on their off night.

Located on Houston's near northeast side on Hirsch Street in the area known as Trinity Gardens, Whispering Pines became one of the most popular black nightclubs in Houston before it closed in the late 1960s. The Houston Public Library Amanda Dixon Branch, built in 1972, currently sits on the lot once occupied by the nightclub.

One thing I started doing was picking up every one of the musicians one by one to take them to the gig. I had to leave the house two or three hours ahead of time to make it to the gig on time. Sometimes girlfriends would have cars and give guys a ride, but nobody else had a car, and I wanted to make sure everybody got there on time.

The first car I had was a 1939 Dodge that Uncle Elmore picked out because he was real good at finding good used cars. I had that car for a while, but my brother L. C. was in the army then and was stationed at Fort Sill in Oklahoma. He came home on a weekend pass and talked me into letting him take that car back up there. Well, he drove that car so hard that he burned it up.

The next car I got was a '49 Ford, and it was a big car. That was the car that I started picking people up in. Before they had them Fender (electric) basses, you had to have that big bass, so you had six of us in one car with that bass right down the middle. We had the drums tied on the roof with the (PA) speakers. I don't know how we did it, but we all loved it and put music first. We used to say "next to mama came music."

This was when I pretty much developed my sound, and most of the sax players around then that wanted to play blues wanted to play like me.

I played a little jazz, but I never was a jazz guy. I've always played the tenor sax, and I got that from Charlie Parker. He said one time that if you play one of 'em (types of saxophones) good enough, you don't have to play no more. Now, it's a whole different story. But I played the oboe and soprano sax in high school, although I never took them on a gig. I always just took the tenor sax. Even today, anybody that's heard me once and hears me again, they'll know it's me and can tell me from any other sax player. I describe my style as being rock 'n' roll bluesy sax. Some people have even said that I'm the king of the rock 'n' roll saxophone.

My style developed from listening to Louis Jordan, Gene Ammons, Stanley Turrentine, and a variety of players, and it just came out the way it came out. If I took a solo, I tried to make it mesh with the way the singer was singing; it might be sweet or honkin'. To get that honkin' tone you have to use a lot of growlin' in your throat and through the mouthpiece while you're blowing, and there's certain things you can do with your lips to make the notes do the things you want them to do. There's a variety of things you can do to get that sound. Whatever sound I'm looking for, I use what I know to change those sounds to get the one I want. It has to do with the way your embouchure is, how hard you blow, how much wind you push in and push out. There's so many tricks to getting the sound you want to come out, and you learn 'em over the years, so after a few years it'll come out almost automatically.

When I first started playing, to get a certain tone I would practice just holding whole notes. I started by holding whole notes tied together for eight beats instead of four. Then I would hold three whole notes for twelve beats and would practice holding those notes together until I got the sound I was comfortable with. You have to work at it, though. You might do it so long that you get tired, so you lay your horn down, and go get something to eat or a good drink of lemonade or something, then come back and try it again.

After I went out on the road, my style developed even more based on who I was playing with. For instance, playing with Sam Cooke, he sang soft and sweet, so I tried to fit the way he was singing. With Little Richard, he sang harsh and growling and wild, so I played honkin', wild sax.

By now Roy was also becoming quite popular on the guitar around

Houston because he could play anything—jazz, blues, you name it—and he could play anything T-Bone Walker could play.

Roy Gaines

I WAS WORKING at Pee Wee's Shoes, across the street from Oakman Cleaners, when Mr. Oakman bought Whispering Pines. Pee Wee told Mr. Oakman that I played guitar, and about this time Grady and the Blues Ramblers started playing at Whispering Pines. I started doing shows there, too, but I didn't play with Grady right at first. We would play what they called floor shows, where Grady's band might back up all the different acts on the show. I started playing on some of those shows and made good money in tips even though I was only about fourteen or fifteen at the time. People were throwing them dollars at me, and sometimes I'd make $5 or $10 a night!

Roy not only became quite a draw around Houston but also got noticed nationally, as he was dubbed "the 14-year-old sensation." He attracted the attention of the publishers of *Ebony/Jet* magazine and was featured in the September 10, 1953, issue of the magazine. The text accompanying a photo of Roy playing guitar and singing read in part, "Although he has been playing the instrument only two years, 14-year-old Texas-born Roy Gaines has been rated by musicians as the most promising young guitarist in the U.S."[1]

Roy went on the road a little before I did. He was only fifteen when he left with Roy Milton and Mickey Champion, who did "RM Blues," which was a pretty big song at the time. Roy wound up playing with Milton for a long time, then from Milton he played with Chuck Willis, and they did quite a few recordings together. He stayed with him until Chuck passed away, then he started playing with Billie Holiday and was based out of New York. After Billie Holiday came Brook Benton, and after that he played with Ray Charles for a long time.

Grady at around age nineteen. Photo from the Grady Gaines Collection.

It was around this time, while I was still in high school, that I got a chance to meet Lightnin' Hopkins. I ran into him after he had started getting big when white folks took him over (began listening to his music). He played them little beer places and rooms by himself. Before you knew anything, everybody was trying to cover his licks. But he played what he felt and put the notes where he wanted to put 'em, so he had no direct way of playing, and a lot of musicians didn't think much about that then. They thought you were supposed to stay with the music—the bars, measures, and notes and so forth.

We also got to see T-Bone Walker a lot in Houston during them days. He was *the man* before B. B. King. He and (Bronze Peacock nightclub and Peacock Studios owner) Don Robey liked to gamble, and sometimes Robey would win what he was gonna pay him to play, so T-Bone would have to play some dates for free. T-Bone was real down-to-earth, from Conroe, you know? When he'd come to town and play at the City Auditorium, there'd be a line of guitar players, and he'd be playing a number and let them all come up on stage and play one at a time. He used to do that with Roy. B. B. would do that, too, but T-Bone did it first. T-Bone really liked Roy, though; used to call him his son. He was a showman, man. His favorite thing to do was play behind his neck and do the splits. He had some real neat showman stuff, and everybody was trying to do what he was doing in some way back then.

Another popular club we played at then was the Club DeLisa on Bennington Street. It was owned by Mr. and Mrs. Branch, and they was real good people. We became the house band there and stayed for a good while. Mr. Branch was a carpenter and plumber and all that and actually built that club himself. It was one of the nicest black clubs in town.

Sometimes he paid us about $5 per man but sometimes only about $2 or $3 each, which was fair, but he made up for it by filling two tubs with beer and ice and put 'em right by the stage, so we played for that $2 or $3 plus all that beer. But when they brought in people like Joe Turner and Smiley Lewis or Nappy Brown, they could afford to pay us more.

The Blues Ramblers was about the most popular band in Houston during this time, and the women was pretty crazy about us. There was one night when a policeman caught me over in French Town in Houston. This was after a gig just before I went out on the road, and I had this girl with me. I always knew how to find me a dark street. Sometimes we'd do it in the front seat, and sometimes I'd get comfortable and get in the back seat. I had this girl in the front seat when the police drove up behind us, got out, and flashed that light on us. He said, "Boy, let me see that hair between your teeth!" Now, I hadn't had my head down there at all, but he was being rough or funny or something, but he wasn't laughing. I said I was just taking her home to her house right over there. Well, I got through talking with him, and he let me go, but that was a close call as far as going to jail for being caught out there.

Down at Peacock Studios

It turned out that Don Robey had been hearing a lot about our band playing at Whispering Pines, so he sent his talent scout and arranger, a guy named Joe Scott, to come out to the club to hear us. That's how we got to be one of the recording studio bands at Peacock.

Robey wanted us to play behind artists he was bringing into town to record, like Earl Forest, Big Walter ("the Thunderbird") Price, Gatemouth Brown—anything he had coming through there that was bluesy and stuff, we could take care of it.

At first, Robey recorded at a studio called ACA Studios before he finished his (own) studio. Sometimes musicians showed up ready to play, but sometimes one of them might be off partying somewhere. Well, Robey would go and find 'im and whoop 'im all the way back to the studio. He felt like he was losing money by them standing him up. I remember this guitar player named Goree Carter, and I had heard that Robey hit him one time. Robey had a record shop and office in the back of the studio, and I heard that he hit Goree so hard that it knocked him through the door of the record shop.

Sometimes people didn't understand how important it was (to be on time for a recording session), but he let 'em know. Don Robey always treated me wonderful, and I never had no problem with him. I always did what he asked on time. Whatever the case may be, I would be right there. He always treated me fair. That's all I can say about him. In my opinion, I wish we had a Robey around here now.

Roy Gaines recalls that Joe Scott, originally from Arkansas, was a talent scout and an in-studio musical arranger for Robey. A sharp dresser, Scott frequented the nightclubs—where Robey rarely ventured—decked out in his signature alligator shoes and dark suits with thin ties, in search of talent to record at Robey's Peacock Studios.

Born in the Fifth Ward in 1903, Don Deadric Robey founded what would become a legendary establishment known as the Bronze Peacock Dinner Club in 1945 on Erastus Street. Through the 1940s and early '50s, the Bronze Peacock earned a reputation as one of the finest black-owned nightclubs in the country by serving fine food and drink and housing a huge performance stage where top-level performers of the day, including T-Bone Walker, Louis Jordan, and Ruth Brown, delighted the audience, which included some of Houston's most sophisticated and well-off blacks. Despite its popularity—and possibly because of it—Robey closed the club in 1953. The club became so popular that even some whites began showing up, a development that ran counter to the segregationist mores of the time, and, as a result, started attracting an increasing amount of interest from the Houston Police Department, as did the club's clandestine, backroom gambling.

After closing the club, Robey, whose mother was white and father was black, turned his attention to recording, booking, and managing some of the talented blues, R&B, and gospel artists in the area at his new Peacock Studios, housed in the same building as the now-departed Bronze Peacock. The first big-time star to record under the Peacock label was Clarence "Gatemouth" Brown, and many others would follow, including Earl Forest, Johnny Ace, Big Walter "the Thunderbird" Price, and Bobby "Blue" Bland. To support those artists, he founded the Buffalo Booking Agency and placed it under the astute direction of Evelyn Johnson, who became a critical figure in the development of Houston blues.

Almost from the beginning, Robey was a polarizing figure among musicians, who either sang his praises or damned him for what many believe was Robey's practice of "cheating" songwriters out of royalty money. Those who knew him say Robey possessed a domineering personality coupled with a quick temper. But it was his dealings with songwriters in particular that caused some to curse him. Although Robey almost certainly took advantage of songwriters who were more interested in scoring some quick cash for a night on the town than they

were in securing copyrights for their songs and waiting to see whether
they would be recorded and make any money, scarce evidence exists
to suggest that Robey engaged in any illegal activity in his dealings
with songwriters. One of these was longtime Texas Upsetter Joe
Medwick, who sold many songs, such as "Further on up the Road,"
recorded by Bland, to Robey for instant cash. Robey would copyright
the songs and assume writer or cowriter credits, usually under his
pseudonym of "Deadric Malone," and later collect the royalties even
though it's highly doubtful that Robey was even a middling songwriter.

Robey's music holdings would eventually include the Peacock,
Duke, Songbird, Back Beat, and Sure-Shot record labels. Upon his
retirement in 1973, he sold his holdings outright to ABC/Dunhill for an
undisclosed sum. Robey died in 1975 at the age of seventy-one.[1]

The first session I can remember playing on at ACA was behind a white
guy. We recorded a 45 with him, but I can't remember his name. This was
around 1953. At that point, we only recorded 45s. We would go in and do
a session where you'd cut two 45s. We would have a booth for the horns
and drums to keep them from bleeding over, but the whole band would
play the whole song at the same time. We didn't go back and do overdubs
much, except for laying the vocals down. If it sounded OK, we'd use that
track. If not, you'd go back and try something else.

Some artists would come into the studio after rehearsing and would
be ready to lay it down, but some bands would go to the studio and do
it on the spot, and that took longer. Don Robey wasn't involved in the
sessions, but he'd be in the control room a lot, listening like a hound dog.
The only time he'd come out was if there was something he wanted in a
certain spot in a song. Most of the time he would talk to the singer about
how he wanted them to express themselves and how he wanted them to
say certain words. Joe Scott would be in there with the musicians, making
sure they were playing the right notes and stuff.

Milton Hopkins, guitarist and Grady's longtime friend

SOMEBODY TOLD ROBEY that they saw a guy sitting on the porch playing a guitar over in Trinity Gardens on Lockwood Street. He decided to ride down Lockwood to see if he could see the guy sittin' on the porch playing guitar, and that's what happened. He stopped, and I thought it was the police, but I knew I hadn't done nothing. I must have been about eighteen or nineteen then. He introduced himself and told me what he was all about, what he was looking for, and what he needed, and I accepted then and there. I went inside, got a big brown paper bag, some shoes, some shaving gear, and a couple pairs of pants. I didn't have no suitcase. I grabbed my guitar and my Silvertone amplifier, and we cut out. There was a lot of stuff going around about Robey, but I never experienced any of that; I just heard about it. It was all hearsay, and when people would start talking about it, I'd back up because if I said anything negative about the man, I wouldn't know what I was talking about. He was always a cordial businessperson with me, but we didn't shuck and jive around like musicians like to do. Maybe that's why I didn't get caught up in that web. My daddy used to tell me, "Son, don't play with the boss."

I'd say the studio at Peacock was medium sized, not a huge studio like some I recorded in later on, but if need be, you could assemble a twelve- to fourteen-piece orchestra in there. It would have been kind of tight, but it could happen. In fact, I'm certain it did because Pluma Davis still had his big band then. Sometimes the sessions happened all night, like a good poker game. You might go into the studio at six in the evening, and sometimes it'd be morning before you got out of there. But it was never boring. The first group I remember recording with was a gospel group. I was not what you'd call a hell of a guitar player at that time, but I'd been told since I started playing that you had to learn all of your chords and pay attention to the rhythm because that was more important than lead (guitar), and that's how I got jobs—by being able to memorize all those patterns. I don't even know how I came up with a lot of those patterns. Some were written, but I didn't read music that well. But I practiced all the time, and that's how I managed to make it with the rhythm thing. Plus, playing with Grady helped. He played with rhythm. The way he played his horn would tell you what he was feeling. But it was weird that I was able to do anything on a session because I couldn't read music well. If you listen to the last album Johnny Ace made, there's a lot of sophisticated stuff going on in there, and I was playing and reading it, but it was still Greek to me. I would have a stack of sheet music in front of me, but I was not a reading musician. It was put in front of me, and I was told to do the best I could. Joe Scott started teaching me how to move chords around and make it say what you want to say at those sessions. He treated me like a reading musician. Whenever the A&R (artist and repertoire) man started handing out them parts, Scott laid 'em on my stand, too.

Robey had the recording studio and the Buffalo Booking Agency in the same building on Erastus Street, and he could even press the records in the back. I recorded behind so many people that it's hard to remember them all. We recorded "Whoopin' and Hollerin'" (Duke, 1953) and "Your Kind of Love" (Duke, 1954) with Earl Forest. We recorded "Dirty Work at the Crossroads" (Peacock, 1952) and "Midnight Hour" (Peacock, 1954) with Gatemouth Brown and "Pack Fair and Square" (Peacock, 1956) and "Shirley Jean" (Peacock, 1955) with Big Walter "the Thunderbird" Price. We also recorded with some of the gospel artists like the Mighty Mighty Clouds of Joy.

By this time, I had switched to playing a Selmer saxophone with a Burt Lawson mouthpiece, and I've been buying Selmers ever since. I had just the one sax when I started touring with Little Richard, but later on I got a bunch of 'em. I got five saxes now. I had six, but I gave one of 'em, a King alto, to a little kid that lived next door. I don't know if he kept playing or not, but I was hoping he would do something with it.

I've got a Selmer Mark VI now, and I love it. I did most of my recording with that, but on the last album *(Jump Start)* we did it with a (Selmer) Super 80. I have a black one, a white one, and two gold ones and a soprano, too. The last two saxes I bought were a black Selmer 80 and a white Super 80, and I got those about fifteen years ago, but they're as good as new. Lester Hill, who played in the Upsetters for a while, fixes my saxes now. He's over at H&H Music. Back in the '50s and '60s, Red Novacs was a salesman at H&H who always looked out for the musicians. I've been dealing with H&H for a long time.

Anyway, at this time, you had clubs on just about every corner in Houston, with live music all over the place. The major clubs were the Gypsy Tea Room, the Eldorado Ballroom, Whispering Pines, Club Ebony, Club DeLisa, Club Matinee, and Shady's Playhouse. You could always find a place to hear some good blues, and they had these jazz jam sessions where there'd be music to cover everybody's tastes. Most of the crowds was all black, but if we were playing where I knew there would be a white audience, I tried to play some songs that I know the white folks would like. For instance, Gatemouth Brown's "Okie Dokie Stomp" was a crossover hit. Blacks and whites loved it.

In my opinion, Houston definitely has its own "sound." I think R&B would stand out here like Chicago blues. On the other hand, people like Lightnin' Hopkins came from here, and didn't nobody play no more blues than he did. You got all these guys that migrated to Chicago—Muddy Waters, Jimmy Reed, Little Walter—so I think they accepted that kind of blues in Chicago more than people did here (Houston). I think down here people accepted blues that was more like R&B because we were recording R&B with Don Robey. More R&B was recorded during that time here than in Chicago. In Chicago, they was more dead on Muddy Waters and that kind of blues. We had more horns here—a bunch of horns. That's what made it R&B when you started adding horns to it.

Like Nothin' They'd Ever Seen

Joe Bell was a good friend of mine who ran with me for a while before he decided to buy a guitar and learn how to play it. At that time, T-Bone Walker was like the only guitar player out there, and anybody that picked up a guitar wanted to play like T-Bone. Joe Bell did, too, and he became a big hit around town because he could play just like T-Bone. He wound up playing with my band for a long time, and we became real good friends.

The Blues Ramblers used to play at a lot of car lots on the weekend, where the band would be broadcast over the radio, and people would come out to buy cars while the band would be playing. Well, Joe had met this white woman—real nice-looking lady—and he started going around town with her for a few months and brought her to one of the car-lot gigs during the day. We were playing at Whispering Pines that night, and Joe's girlfriend said she had a pretty white girl for me to meet later, but I had something else to do, and I couldn't be with that girl that night.

Joe's girl showed up at Whispering Pines for our show, and while we were playing, the police came into the club. They took Joe off the stage and beat him up terrible. I was lucky because I would have been right there with him if that white girl had been there for me. Joe stayed in jail for a couple of nights, and his girlfriend went down and bailed him out. Right after he got out of jail, we had another gig to play, but I had to turn his guitar up and down for him because he couldn't hear because they had beat him up so bad. He's lucky they didn't kill him.

Houston could be pretty rough back then, but you wouldn't have no problems (with white people) if you knew where you were at and acted accordingly, and that's what I did. I mean, if you know fire's gonna burn you, you ain't gonna stick your hand in it. I tried to live my whole life like that, and that's why I've lasted as long as I have. I had a lot of close calls, but me handling myself the way I did helped to prolong my life. Joe messin' with that white woman in public just brought too much attention to himself.

About this same time (1953), Little Richard was playing a lot around town with this band called Raymond Taylor and the Tempo Toppers. He did that for a few years. The group was Taylor playing trombone and keyboards and his wife, Mildred, playing drums. Richard was one of the singers, along with Gil Moore, the bass singer, and Jimmy Swann and Billy Brooks. They played a lot at the Club Matinee and all over the South—Oklahoma, Mississippi, Alabama, Georgia—but Houston was their base because they was being booked by the Buffalo Booking Agency.

The Tempo Toppers were real popular in Houston because Richard was like nothin' people had ever seen. They played a lot of places, like the Whispering Pines and the Anchor Room, and they played a lot of the after-hours shows, too. After the big-name acts would play their shows, they would go back to the hotel and party and jam, so everybody would flop there. That's where I first met Richard, but he had heard me at Peacock Studios. I sat in with the Tempo Toppers one night at the Anchor Room, and shortly after that, Richard had decided to leave the Tempo Toppers and go out on his own. Robey had already started recording him and Gil Moore and Billy Brooks, but Richard was already becoming a hit because he was out front of the Tempo Toppers. We recorded a couple of songs with the Tempo Toppers back then, one called "Fool at the Wheel" and a tune called "Rice, Red Beans, and Collard Greens," but they wasn't hits or anything. But when we played a town, and if they hadn't already heard it, after they heard us play it, it sold like crazy and became the number-one hit in that town.

Richard asked me to play some dates with him in Oklahoma, Georgia, Dallas, and different places, but this was before he had made any recordings that were hits, although he had recorded some mediocre things at Peacock. My first impression of Richard was that he was something really different, and the people just loved him. I thought the world of him and thought he was a star that was going to be an even bigger star.

The Blues Ramblers was still real popular all over town, and we had all sorts of women following us wherever we played, and they would be so sweet and fine that you just couldn't hardly resist. I remember one time we was playing at the Eldorado Ballroom, and this man wanted to kill me over his girlfriend. I had taken his girl, and we had sex in the car, and he saw us coming back into the club. The band was still playing, but it was near the end of the gig, so I left the stage and had to back up all the way out the door from the bar at the front, through all the people and out the door. I kept my eyes on him the whole time. I think he had a gun, but I wasn't sure. I kept looking at him, and he kept looking at me as I backed down the steps and jumped into my car. Somebody else was driving, and we got the hell out of there. That was a real close call that was right before "Tutti Frutti" hit, and I went on the road with Richard.

But before "Tutti Frutti" became a hit, Richard did a lot of recording at Peacock Studios for Don Robey, but I know Richard and Robey had some problems.

In *The Life and Times of Little Richard: The Authorised Biography by Charles White* (London: Omnibus Press, 1984, 37), Richard said his constant challenging of Robey's authority resulted in several clashes. He recalled a specific confrontation with the no-nonsense studio boss:

Little Richard

HE JUMPED ON ME, knocked me down and kicked me in the stomach. It gave me a hernia that was painful for years. I had to have an operation. Right there in the office he beat me up. Knocked me out in the first round. Wasn't no second or third round; he just come around that desk and I was down! He was known for beating people up, though. He would beat up everybody except Big Mama Thornton. He was scared of her. She was built like a big bull.

Richard liked the way Clifford and I played because we played so good together. Clifford and I had a sound that no other two tenor players in that time had. It wasn't often in rhythm and blues and rock 'n' roll that there was two tenor players (in a band). Gene Ammons and Sonny Stitt, they had their sound, but they were playing jazz. But now Clifford and I had a sound that everybody was talking about. I mean *all* the musicians was talking about it. We had a hell of a sound together, but we did a lot of practicing together. We'd practice all day and cook up red beans and rice and stuff and keep right on practicing. That was before we went to meet Richard. Then after we joined him, we just kept on practicing, but we really put that sound together before we went out there on the road. So when Richard sent for us to join his band, it wasn't no sweat for us to learn his songs because we'd been playing 'em for so long.

Gaines and Burks would continue their musical collaboration for nearly three decades until the 1970s, when both men left the road behind. Burks eventually settled in New York, where he continued to play locally throughout the 1990s. Now retired and not in the best of health, Burks and Gaines remained good friends and talked frequently to reminisce about the old days and the many stages and experiences they shared as members of the Upsetters. Burns passed away in October 2014 at age 84.

Clifford played a little different than I did. He played a little bit more jazzier and a little bit smoother. I always wanted my own sound, so my sound was like between Illinois Jacquet and Arnett Cobb, and Clifford, he had a big tone—course we both had big tones—but his was smoother than what I played. So we took those two sounds and put them together, and that's what made it so good.

Plus practicing together all the time, when we'd make a run, if I get that first note, whatever note I have, whatever note he get, we just automatically go on into it—into whatever we'd be playing. See, when you practice together a lot like that, you know what each other's doing, and wherever one go, the other one knows where to go to match it. It seemed like we were born to make music together.

Dancin' and Steppin'

After Grady and Clifford joined Little Richard's Upsetters in 1955, they immediately set out on a whirlwind life of constant touring. The Upsetters stayed out on the road for the better part of three years. The touring ended only when Little Richard suddenly left the music business to enter the ministry in December 1957. When Grady and Clifford met Richard in Maryland to join the Upsetters, three to four months had passed since they had last seen the singer in Houston.

Lots of things happened in those three years, like when we were going from Los Angeles to Australia, we stopped in Hawaii and had dinner, and we could see all the different sights and take pictures. We stopped in the Fiji Islands and did the same thing. We always tried to make it like a vacation until we got to the job, when we'd take care of business. But we never did just do nothing. We always tried to make it as exciting as we could.

So if we had time, maybe three or four days or something between shows, we'd just make it like a trip, like vacation. We'd stop and get us something to eat and stop on the side of the road in a park or someplace and just do sightseeing.

Once we got to where the job was, we got some time to stay over and get up the next morning, eat breakfast, and get prepared. If you got time to get to the next gig, that's what we would do. But sometimes you would have a long ways to go, and you would have to leave from one gig and go straight to the next job, so you had to allow for that time and just keep on steppin'.

Everywhere we went it was jam-packed and overflowing. They had to turn people away. People were fainting, and they had to carry so many different girls and women off just about every gig we played. After a show, we'd feel wonderful. We'd be wringing wet with sweat, but we felt great. It's a good feeling, nothing like it, really. When you got a crowd that's really going for it like that, ain't no better feeling.

Each show would be about an hour and a half, but it might be two different shows in a night. Now, Richard wouldn't do too much over an hour unless he had the crowd going. He'd go all night long as long as that crowd was in there. But just the regular way of doing it was about an hour, hour and fifteen minutes, something like that.

But it all depended on how long we would keep one song going, 'cause we could get on one song and keep it going for thirty minutes. That's the way he did it. If we got 'em going, if we got the people going, you just lay there with them until you feel like you want to let 'em go. Then you let go and go off into something else even more exciting.

Chuck Connor, Upsetters drummer

WE WOULD HIT THE BANDSTAND around nine o'clock and play 'til about eleven thirty, then take a one-hour intermission. We'd go back on and play another hour, so we might play for three and a half hours altogether, but we had enough material to do that. We'd do some instrumentals, Lee Diamond might sing for about a half an hour, then Richard would hit the bandstand. We didn't just play Richard's songs; we'd play other songs that were popular at the time, too.

Playing at the City Auditorium in Houston was a big night for me. It was always a dream of mine to play at the City Auditorium, and I got to do that early on with the Upsetters. Richard liked for the saxes to walk all over the building, so we got to doing one of them hot rockin' tunes, and we set out walking around all through the crowd. We had plenty of strut back then, so there would be two or three of us on the floor while the others kept the riff going onstage.

We put on a hell of a show, and it was a sellout, and some of my family made it, too. After that show, I felt like I had accomplished one of my goals, but I wanted to go further. The next thing was to play the Apollo Theater in New York, then the next thing was to play overseas, which we did. Man, I was living my dream.

We always tried to leave in time to allow enough time for us to make it to the next gig. That's what we always tried to do, but it didn't always work out that way. I remember one time we was on the New Jersey turnpike, and we pulled into a tollbooth to pay the toll to go through, and when we pulled in there, the station wagon just stopped. The timing chain was out. So we had to push it over to the side and try to call to see if we could rent one (a vehicle) to get us into the job. So that was one hard time we had there to try to make that job. We made it, but we was a little late.

One time the driver dozed off, and we ran off into a cotton field. That was down in Georgia. Nobody got hurt, but we was lucky that it was flat ground, you know; it wasn't no deep ditch. But we spent all that day in that cotton field. Several things like that happened. We had our share of those kind of incidents. I always believed that when you leave in time, you allow yourself time for anything that happens so you won't miss that job. That's the way I always believed, and I do it right now. Although the musicians don't like that because they believe in getting there (at the) last minute. You know, they wanna get their last minute at home or whatever they doing. But that ain't the way I do it.

Another close call happened when I was riding with Richard. I used to ride with him and his driver and Audrey, who was this woman Richard was talking about marrying for a while. I was riding in the front seat, and we were going from Dallas to Amarillo or some place in West Texas. We left after the gig and was driving in the early morning. Richard was driving on this long strip of highway when the sun started coming up.

Well, Richard got sleepy and had run off his side of the road into the other side, and one of them big trucks was coming. I happened to wake up, grabbed the wheel, and hollered, "Richard!" He woke up, but I pulled us back into our lane, and that was a close one. That could've been it right there. But we had a lot of close calls out there, so there must have been a lot of prayin' mamas and family back home that helped us pull through.

Grady on stage with Little Richard at the Apollo Theater in New York, circa 1956. Photo from the Grady Gaines Collection.

But when you're out there on that road, 365 days a year for twenty-five years, that's some time on your behind, but that's what I did, and there wasn't no stoppin' because I was doing what I loved to do.

There was an incident we had in Long Beach, where we was there playing a show, and we checked into the hotel. We come back out, and the whole van was stripped; everything in it was gone. That same thing happened to us in Tulsa, Oklahoma. Most of the time, the cats would take their instruments to their room—all but the drums and sound system. But back in those days, you didn't hardly have TVs in the room, and you could only stay at the black hotels. We would carry our TVs and record players along with us. All that stuff got stolen, but I gotta say that's just a part of it. You win some and lose some.

Looking to capitalize on the young people's growing fascination with the new musical art form called rock 'n' roll, Hollywood producers released three hastily put-together movies featuring some of the biggest early rock 'n' roll hit makers, including Little Richard and the Upsetters. The first movie, *The Girl Can't Help It*, released on December 1, 1956, is generally regarded as the best of the three. With busty starlet Jayne Mansfield serving as eye candy, the movie, directed by Frank Tashlin, tells the story of a down-and-out gangster who hires an alcoholic press agent to turn his blonde-bombshell girlfriend (Mansfield) into a recording star despite her obvious lack of talent. The movie wasn't exactly Oscar bait, and the real stars of the film were the musical acts that performed, including Little Richard and the Upsetters, Fats Domino, Gene Vincent, and the Platters.

The second movie was released just a couple of weeks after *The Girl Can't Help It. Don't Knock The Rock*, released on December 14, 1956, and directed by Fred F. Sears, features disc jockey Alan Freed, the man generally credited with creating the term "rock 'n' roll," along with performances from the likes of Richard and the Upsetters and Bill Haley and the Comets.

It was during this movie that Gaines jumped on top of Richard's piano, creating an instant buzz around the nation and providing the rock

Iconic image of Grady on top of Little Richard's piano from the film *Don't Knock the Rock* (1956). Photo from the Grady Gaines Collection.

'n' roll audience with the first glimpse of the athleticism that would mark Gaines's onstage performances throughout his career. It happened while he was blowing the scorching solo to "Long Tall Sally" (credited to Lee Allen on the Specialty Records recording), and the still shot of Gaines on the piano has become an iconic image from rock's early days that personified the youthful, no-holds-barred attitude of the rebellious new music.

The last movie, *Mr. Rock 'n' Roll,* released in October of 1957 and directed by Charles S. Dubin, was for all intents and purposes an early concert film, as the plot was even more forgettable than that of *Don't Knock the Rock.*[1]

We did all right with the movies. When it came time for us to do our cut, we just did the number onstage while they filmed it. It was the same for all three of 'em. There wasn't no talking parts or anything like Elvis Presley had in his movies. That kind of thing hadn't gotten out there yet in 1956, where if you were black, you could be in a movie with Jayne Mansfield, except as a performer.

That scene in *Don't Knock the Rock* where I jump on top of Richard's piano during my solo has followed me throughout my life. I think I had done that at least one time before, and I didn't do it at every show, but I would do it every now and then, and the crowd always got off on it. I remember doing it later when we were playing at the Apollo Theater. What I was trying to do was put a little more into the song because Richard was shakin' and jumpin' and doing all sorts of stuff, so I just got up and did something, too. It was totally spontaneous. Richard would holler and keep on beating them keys, and I kept right on soloing up there until I jumped down off the piano and kept on playing and kept the momentum going. I was the only one doing that, but the other sax players would be walking through the crowd. We could give each other a break because we had those five saxes in the band.

There weren't no wireless microphones back then, of course. The guitar and bass had amps, and the piano went through the (sound) board, but the horn section had mics on stands in front of us. You had to learn

Grady on top of Little Richard's piano, with the Upsetters in background, from the film *Don't Knock the Rock* (1956). Photo from the Grady Gaines Collection.

how to work the bell where the sound comes out and move it around the mic, which helped you get different sounds, too, like a singer has to do with the mic. When I got on top of Richard's piano, I usually just walked away from the mic, but sometimes I would stick a microphone down inside the horn. If somebody on stage knew I was gonna do it, they might stick a mic down the horn, but sometimes I got up there and didn't have nothing. I would just be blowin' and wigglin' so the crowd knew I was blowin' but couldn't exactly hear everything I was doing.

Aside from the occasional life-threatening traveling mishap or loss of property, the majority of Gaines's life on the road with Little Richard and the Upsetters was an endless blur of highways, airports,

49

cheap motels, rooming houses, and almost nightly gigs. For the most part, traveling through the East and West Coasts, the band endured a limited number of racially charged incidents, but playing in the South was a whole different matter.

When we were doing a tour in the South, we had some problems, but on the East Coast we didn't have no problems. One thing that happened a lot in the South was when you'd be driving for a long time and you needed to stop and get some gas or get something to eat, you would see the light on at a gas station down the road, so you'd pull over. But once you pulled in, and the owner could see that we was black, they'd turn the lights off and act like they was closed. Happened all the time in the South.

I remember one time we got stopped by police with Richard outside of Detroit. We stopped to get a hamburger, and he (Richard) ate part of the hamburger, but we were running late for that gig, so he put the part he didn't eat in a bag and threw it out the window. We were about a few miles from Detroit, where we were gonna play, and about a mile down the road (from where the bag was thrown) when the cops stopped us and made Richard walk back to pick it up. They told him they were gonna arrest him if he didn't go pick it up, so he walked backed there and picked it up while they watched him.

We were playing for mixed (race) crowds all over the world because the music didn't have no color if you worked for a crossover artist like Richard. Once rock 'n' roll came out, things changed because more whites started crossing over with black performers. But we played lots of gigs, mostly in the South, where they segregated the crowds, and sometimes the headliner would refuse to play unless they let them all come together. Sometimes you'd have the whites upstairs and blacks downstairs or the other way around. Sometimes they'd have a rope between them, but when they got to dancing they would migrate together.

We didn't just stand there and play. We were moving around, walking the floor through the audience; we'd do a little something of everything, including me playing on top of the piano. I wish I could do that now!

Every band out there would come out and watch us and started doing them (dance) steps and stuff. We were the leaders, the groundbreakers in playing rock 'n' roll for two decades or more.

Even though we were traveling so much, we still practiced. We would practice in hotel rooms mostly. Like if it's something we wanted to learn or a new song came out, a hot song that was really being heard, we would call the musicians to the room. A lot of times we wouldn't set up the whole band, we'd just get maybe the keyboards or the guitar player or the bass and some horns and get in them rooms and learn 'em like that. Then when we'd get to the gig, we'd basically have the tune, but we'd go over it again with the whole band. So we did a lot of rehearsing like that.

Sometimes you got some days off or even a week off, and we could set up and rehearse with the whole group. Again, it all depends on how important what we had to learn was. If it was something really important, we'd make room for rehearsal that we had to do at a certain time.

But we didn't have no charts (sheet music). No, our charts were in our heads, but we had some up there, let me tell ya. The only time we had charts was if we were going through the circuit of theaters like the Apollo or the Paramount in Brooklyn, the Royal in Baltimore, the Uptown in Philadelphia, the Howard in DC, or the Regal in Chicago, when we had to play behind the whole show with other groups. Then we would have to read the charts for the other acts. So that's when we would have to read, but for Richard's music we didn't have to do no reading.

If we were gonna play behind a whole show, we would have to read the rest of the show's music. They would have their music, and a majority of them had their own rhythm section. They would give us the horns' (charts) or whoever needed the music, and we would read it. That happened a whole lot of times.

For Richard's music, sometimes I came up with the horn parts, or the other horn players might come up with it. Whoever come up with something, if it fit good, then the rest of them would fall in. We might do it two or three times, about two or three nights, and we'd have it, we'd have a jam. That's how we did that. We kinda knew what each other's gonna do, and we caught it spontaneous. It would just fall right in, and it would work.

Because I had played with Richard for a while, our music just sort of married together, and we felt each other automatically almost. His style of playing and my style of playing just fell right in there. For example, when we recorded "Keep a-Knockin'" he just started singing and playing, and I put the riff in there, and the rest of the band just fell in behind. We just happened to be two people who felt the same way in the music thing. That's the way I see it.

The Upsetters' relentless touring schedule all but prevented Gaines from returning to Houston for more than a few days or even hours at a time, but he and the rest of the band were treated to the comforts of home by Grady's older brother, L. C. Gaines, whenever a tour took them to California. L. C., who was employed for years on the Ford Motor Company assembly line, and his wife, Shirley, lived at various times in Compton, San Pedro, and Long Beach, but wherever they resided, Grady and brother Roy would make their way to L. C.'s house for some legendary throwdowns. Grady's older sister, Reba, and her husband, Elijah, also lived in Southern California at the time, so their home became a gathering spot as well.

We couldn't wait to get to California because we knew we were gonna party, and L. C. and Shirley would show us the best time of our lives every time we went there. Everything we even thought we wanted, they had it, and L. C. is one of the best barbecuers in the world. Plus, they had all kinds of drink, women, you name it. It was so much fun.

Sometimes we would go to my sister Reba and her husband Elijah's house, and she threw some humdingers, too. They had a swimming pool, and they got the house all ready for us. As soon as I hit town, Reba gave me the keys to her new Cadillac! And Reba met 'em all (Little Richard, Sam Cooke, Little Willie John). She was a go-getter! Everywhere we went in California, they (L. C. and Reba) were right there with us. Most of the time, me and Roy wouldn't be there at the same time, but every now and then we would meet up out there.

They played a big part in our lives by keeping us happy and strong to keep going on that road. All of my sisters and brothers and Mama and

Daddy never did try to stop us from playing music. They always encouraged us, so you couldn't find no brothers and sisters no tighter than we were back in those days. We always looked out for each other. We still do even though we're all up in age now.

L. C. Gaines

I WOULD BE AWFUL GLAD when they came through there. I would also try to make every one of their shows if they were playing a date around LA, Salinas, or Burbank. One time when Grady came through with Little Willie John, he (Little Willie John) told one of them girls I was his manager. I tell you what, Little Richard was a good fella, too. Me and him got along great. He used to open up a suitcase and tell me to get money out. He didn't count it or nothing—just told me to reach in and get something because he wanted to pay me for the barbecue and everything.

Roy Gaines

THOSE WERE SOME REAL GOOD DAYS. We were young and full of energy. When you got your health, ain't nothing better than that. You feeling good, having fun doing everything you want to do; you can't beat it. When I think of those days, I think that's the real reason you got into music. When you're living in those days, you don't think they'll ever end, but here we are looking back on 'em.

The tales of Little Richard's sexual escapades are the stuff of legend, including bizarre practices with men and women and marathon, almost nightly, postconcert orgies. While Richard was widely known

to be bisexual, the rest of the Upsetters were decidedly heterosexual, and the life of a constantly touring musician brought with it an endless stream of willing partners in every city the band visited.

The entire band was involved, but some of the band members would have their own little party. At the end of every show, my room was always full of women. I mean, pretty as they get and as fine as they get, and everybody that didn't have a woman would flock to my room. If they had women, they would leave their room, take the women they have back to their room, then come to my room.

Richard had his thing going, and if I wanted to go down to his room, I'd go down there and maybe just show my face or just to go down there to see what's going on. But I didn't have too much time to see what was going on because I had so much going on in my room!

This happened every night. *Every night.* But you do that for so long 'til you don't wanna see no people. Sometimes we'd be off, or we'd be done playing a pretty long tour, and we'd go and check in, but we're gonna be off three or four days. I would just lock up in my room and didn't come out, no calls, no nothing. Some of the other cats were the same way. You get to seeing people all the time, every day, everywhere you move. I mean, you appreciate that, but you just get tired. But sometimes the women would still get in to see you.

I was in New York and had just had an appendix operation. I came home to Houston to have the operation and stayed there until I got practically well. Then when I went back to New York—we were at the Cecil Hotel, that's where the band stayed, and the rest of the band was already there—and when they (female fans) found out I was there, there was about four or five women who came up to my room, and they actually raped me. I mean, they started taking off their clothes, and they actually did it. I didn't regret it, though!

You see, me and Clifford was the two in that band that got all the women. The others would get some, but I'm talking every night we're getting two or three women or whatever we wanted. So they was jealous over that, and you could tell that they had something in the back of their minds. (Road manager) Henry Nash would always try to push Lee Diamond and them over us because, when we were onstage, all the girls were hollering at me and Clifford and pulling on us and stuff. But we were some good-looking boys, and around New York they used to call me the black Rudolph Valentino. I remember Clifford had this suit with a bunch of rhinestones all over it, and Elvis saw him wearing it and had him some stuff made with all them rhinestones. When we played them clubs around there, it wasn't just black girls, it was all kinda girls, all colors.

Chuck Connor, Upsetters' drummer

WE WERE THE FIRST BAND to have women throwing their panties on stage. That didn't start with Tom Jones, you know? My father told me before I left home, "If you can learn to play those drums, it'll be your passport around the world, and you'll have more women than you can shake a stick at." You know how many women I've slept with? Fifteen hundred in my career from age fifteen until about forty-seven, when I got remarried. Grady might have the same amount; he might have more. You see, there wasn't no AIDS in those days—only gonorrhea and syphilis— and I never did catch any of that. Women would come to the hotel; sometimes you'd have two or three in your room, and you couldn't take care of all of 'em. It seemed like a dream. But in those days everything was free and innocent.

Any town we'd go in, when the show was over, all I had to do was point at which one I wanted, then point her to around the back of the stage, and there it is. She'd meet you backstage, and you'd give her your room number.

Sometimes you'd have three or four women at a time, but what can you really do with that? You might get your thing off two or three times, but then you ain't got nothing but hot air if you can even get it up. It was just something to say, like "I did this or I did that." I mean, you'd be wanting to, but you ain't got nothing left at that moment.

GENE BURKS   Pers. Mgr.   T.P. PRODUCTION INC.
                          Henry Nash   200 W. 57th Street #
                                          New York, N.Y. 10019
                                          LT-1-0922

**Clifford Burks, who also went by the name Gene Burks, in his rhinestone suit in the early '60s.
Photo from the Grady Gaines Collection.**

I also turned many a band member on to women when I'd get out of bed with 'em and let them get in and screw 'em. One time I did that with our guitar player, and that girl wanted to kick my ass. She was serious, too. I had brought her back from the gig, and me and the guitar player were sharing a room, but he had left because he knew I wanted to take her in there and screw her. He asked me to let him get a little, and I said, "OK, OK." We had been drinking and stuff, and when I got through, and I had wore her out, and she had wore me out, she went to sleep. But I eased out of the bed so I wouldn't wake her up, and he eased into the bed. Well, she woke up when he was on top of her because he was a little heavier than me. Man, when she woke up, whoo wee! She was mad as hell and mean. But I managed to cool her down and got away from her.

In Cincinnati one time, there was this cute little black girl that I met when we were doing a show. I had kept her all night after the show, but her parents were looking for her in the morning, so they called the police. When they found her, she was trying to get a cab to go home, and we had just left town, so they didn't catch me. If they had, I would have been in big trouble because she was underage—only about seventeen—and I was about twenty or twenty-one at the time.

I even started to bring a girl back home with me from Australia. This was when we were on the tour where Richard eventually quit music (1957). I had met this pretty little white girl and was going to bring her back home and marry her, but I didn't do it. I got cold feet for fear of what could have happened in the States in the 1950s.

Later, in the '60s some time, I did bring two Canadian girls back home and kept 'em here for a while. I put them up in an apartment, but I got tired of it and let 'em go back. They was two foxes—white girls—and they got little jobs as waitresses or bartenders or something and was bringing in some money. I wasn't pimping them; I never liked to pimp, but if I needed some money, you got to get it for me and give it to me, or we're gonna go our separate ways. Back in those days I needed some money after coming off the road broke.

I made the most money that I ever made playing music when we were with Richard. We used to get rooms for $5 a night, and you know what a room costs now? He was paying us $125 a week, but we could do so much more with it back in the 1950s than you could now. It wouldn't be nothing now. Clifford and I would save around $75 (a week). Him and I doubled up in the same room a lot, and he sent money back to his mama, and I sent mine back to my mama, and she'd put it in the bank for me. She was taking care of my son, Grady Gaines Jr., because I was on the road, so she would keep whatever she needed out of that money to take care of him, and I knew that would be a big help to her.

So when we come back through Houston, we had some money in the bank. If you got to where you could put some of that to the side, then that would be the thing to do, and you kinda come out all right. So we saved some money, but at the time, when you're in the middle of it, it didn't seem like the fun would ever end.

Road Warriors

We was on a tour in Australia in 1957 with Eddie Cochran, Gene Vincent, Jimmy Clinton, and the Big Bopper when Richard told us he was going to quit the business. He was always telling us, "You better save your money because I'm getting out of this business. I'm gonna be a preacher." We didn't take him serious because he would always say that. We were on a bus on a ferry when he said he was gonna throw all of his rings and jewelry into the ocean. He started to do it, and me and Clifford wrestled with him, but he overpowered us and threw them out the window. Now, to me, I think if God gives you a gift, you do your best to carry that out, plus he had a band and people depending on him, so I didn't think he should have left at the time.

Richard was the first "King of Rock 'n' Roll" by a long shot, so when he quit, he gave up his crown. By dropping out, the crown was up for grabs, and Elvis grabbed it, but his (Richard's) religion just led him to do it, so when we got back to the United States, that was it; he quit.

In *The Life and Times of Little Richard: The Authorised Biography* by Charles White, Richard reveals that the Australian tour in 1957 still had another ten days of concerts scheduled, but he refused to play any of the dates and demanded that plane tickets back to the United States be purchased for the entire entourage. As a result, Richard left millions of dollars in cancellations on the table, which prompted several lawsuits to be filed over the matter.

True to his word, shortly after arriving back in the States, Richard entered the Oakwood Seminary in Huntsville, Alabama, where he began studies to become a minister in the Seventh Day Adventist Church. He began singing gospel music, and in 1959 he signed with a Los Angeles agency to schedule a gospel tour. Later that year, he signed a recording contract with Gone Records. But after three years of struggling to adjust to life in the seminary and being out of the public eye, including trying, unsuccessfully, to say good-bye to all of the hedonistic trappings that come with fame, Richard returned to rock 'n' roll, and in 1962 he signed on to perform on a tour of England.[1]

For the Upsetters, Richard's departure, although not completely unexpected, left them without their leader and superstar attraction. But Richard's earlier decision to buck the practice employed by many contemporary singers, such as Chuck Berry, of hiring backing musicians wherever they happened to be playing in favor of working with the same band night in and night out proved beneficial not only for his career but also for the Upsetters as well, who became well known for their outstanding musicianship and wild stage antics. Consequently, when Richard stepped away, the Upsetters were not left completely out in the cold.

We already had a tour of California booked when we got back, so the promoter, Charles Sullivan, got together with Henry Nash, and Dee Clark's name came up. We'd heard about Clark and sent for him from Chicago. He could sing like Little Richard; he had that kind of voice, so we played that whole tour with him up and down the West Coast. Nash told us later that Richard came to a date in Santa Rosa, California, and sat in his car trying to make up his mind if he wanted to come back in, but he didn't do it. We didn't know he was out there until later. I guess he gave his word, so he had to go on and do what he had to do, but he wanted to come back in. That's what I think. But I think he said, "I wanted to be here, so here I am." He'd given his life to God.

After Richard quit, he gave me permission to keep using the name "the Upsetters." We stayed popular because everybody wanted our band, and when artists knew we was behind them, they started getting happy. I'm talking about number-one artists during those days.

Born Delecta Clark in Blytheville, Arkansas, in 1938, Dee Clark grew up in Chicago and enjoyed some minor chart successes with the Chicago group the Goldentones (later called the Kool Gents). The group, under the management of Chicago DJ Herb "the Kool Gent" Kent, who gave them their new moniker, landed a recording deal with Vee-Jay Records and released their debut single "This Is the Night" in 1956. The Chicago label's management convinced Clark to go solo around 1957, but he struggled to find a niche and even mimicked Little Richard's singing style to a degree on his 1958 single "Oh, Little Girl," which did not enjoy any chart success. Following his brief tenure with the Upsetters, Clark returned to Chicago and began to come into his own as a solo artist with the release of "Nobody but You" in 1958. The song climbed to number twenty-one on the pop charts and number three on the R&B chart. "Hey, Little Girl," released in 1959, reached number twenty on the pop chart and the number-two spot on the R&B chart. After the massive success of "Raindrops," a number-two hit on the Billboard chart in 1961, Clark was never able to recapture the success of his earlier hits, but he continued to perform into the 1980s. He died of a heart attack at age fifty-two in 1990.[2]

After Little Richard exited the scene, the Upsetters were soon in need of a guitar player due to a tragic event that claimed the life of Nathaniel Douglas, who had been playing guitar in the band for years, which opened the door for Grady's childhood friend Milton Hopkins to join the band on guitar. A cousin of blues legend Lightnin' Hopkins, Milton recorded with numerous artists at Peacock Studios in the 1950s. Milton didn't get to meet his famous relative, however. His father took him to a Fourth Ward nightclub to hear Lightnin' Hopkins play, but Milton recalls that a big fight broke out before he could meet the legend.

Milton began playing guitar during high school and toured briefly with Peacock artists Johnny Ace and Big Mama Thornton. That tour came to a tragic end when Ace killed himself in 1955 while, according to legend, he was playing a game of Russian roulette. Following a stint in the military, Hopkins wound up playing in the Upsetters from 1958 until around 1963. He then embarked on a career that included an illustrious run as a guitarist and bandleader with B. B. King in the 1960s and early '70s before he returned to Houston in the late '70s.

Nathaniel Douglas got killed by his mother-in-law after she shot him in the back. What I heard was she had his daughter in some club off the Eastex Freeway (in Houston), and he went in to get his daughter out, and when he was walking away, the mother-in-law shot him in the back. He stayed paralyzed for a while before he died. After he got shot was when I talked to Milton.

Milton Hopkins

THEY NEEDED A GUITAR PLAYER, so Grady called me from El Paso and asked me if I was interested in going on the road with the band. I had just gotten out of the army, and I told Grady that I hadn't got my strength back up for playing, but he said come on out, and let's see what happens. I wound up staying there until 1963. My whole situation changed after I joined the Upsetters, and for a while it didn't seem like I was going to be able to cut it with the band. That style of music wasn't new to me, but I had never delved into it. It was rhythm and blues with a lot of rock involved, and they were doing all kinds of routines and steps onstage, and I hadn't been doing that. It was a really flashy and glamorous outfit, and everybody was full of pep and energy. But through listening and practicing, it all worked out. Actually, my playing kind of changed the whole style of the band, and everybody liked it. I played a lot of big chords that would make a six-piece band sound like a twelve-piece, so we had a big, rockin' sound.

We kept Clark on as a singer, but by this time Little Willie John had a hit with "Fever," and Charles Sullivan had booked a tour for him, so we wound up playing a California tour with him. We did the tour with both

The Upsetters in the early 1960s. From left, Grady, Henry Nash, Larry Lanier, Milton Hopkins, Emil Russell, O. C. "Bassie" Robertson, Lee Diamond. Photo courtesy of the Milton Hopkins Collection.

of them, and Clark stayed with us for a while before he went back to Chicago and went on his own and recorded "Raindrops" and "Hey, Little Girl" and all that stuff. He already had a recording deal with Vee-Jay Records out of Chicago, and we recorded one tune, "Every Night about This Time," a tune Little Richard also recorded, with Dee.

We were working with Universal Attractions out of New York by this time, and we kept on touring with Little Willie John and didn't miss a beat. Little Willie John was a wonderful little young guy but was sort of wild. He was so young and had all them big hits and that big voice. We were real close. His wife and kids was like family to me and the band, and I liked Little Willie John a lot, but he was a little wild and carried it overboard. When we made it back to Houston, Little Willie John used to love to get some barbecue at the Kozy Kitchen on Lockwood. He would buy three or four boxes of barbecue and head to the hotel, where we'd party with all different types of girls and eat and drink and do everything else all night. When you young, you do a lot of silly things that you wouldn't do after you grow older if you wise up. But I've got nothing but good things to say about him, and I like to look at the good side. He was just young and wild like most young people. I was pretty wild myself, but you either wake up, or you're gonna go by the wayside if you keep doing what you used to.

Milton Hopkins

> LITTLE WILLIE JOHN was an energetic little fellow and a hell of a singer. When he was on that stage, he had everybody's attention. But he was a young guy and did what young guys do. Because everything was new to him, he did plenty of everything all the time. He did have a temper on him, too, and we got a little taste of it in Baltimore when he got into a fight with a lawyer on a gig. That almost got all of us in trouble because, when the police showed up, they weren't just looking for Little Willie John, they were looking for the whole band, but they didn't take us (to jail). But he definitely had a temper, and he was very sensitive about his size. As popular as he was, being called Little Willie John, I don't think he liked it.

From 1956 through '61, Little Willie John (born William Edward John in Cullendale, Arkansas) had fourteen hits on the R&B and pop charts, the biggest of which was his first charting song, "All around the World," a revised version of the Titus Turner song that reached number five on the Billboard chart. "Fever," released in 1956, reached number twenty-four on the pop chart and sold more than one million copies. It was famously covered by Peggy Lee in 1958, and it would become her signature song for the remainder of her recording and performing career, but it also brought a level of renewed fame and recognition to John. Other hits by John include "Need Your Love So Bad" (1955) and "Talk to Me, Talk to Me" (1958).[3]

But in addition to his soaring voice, John also possessed a quick temper that belied his charming, fun-loving public persona and a propensity to consume alcohol in mass quantities. This potent mix led to several incidents and caused his record company to drop him in 1963. In 1966 John was convicted of manslaughter for killing a man in a knife fight after a show in Seattle. He was incarcerated at the Washington State Penitentiary, where he died at age thirty in 1968. The cause of death was officially listed as heart attack, but members of his family challenged that ruling, believing that he had died under suspicious circumstances. His was inducted into the Rock and Roll Hall of Fame in 1996.[4]

By this time, the Upsetters had become the hottest band out there, and we stayed that way for over two decades. There was a show at the Apollo we played with Little Willie John, and there were about ten other acts on there, but Little Willie John was the star. I think we played three or four shows a day and five shows on Saturday. We had a song that me and Clifford put together called "The Upsetter," and every time we played that song, people would just go crazy, with girls jumping onstage and stuff. Our band would come on first before Little Willie John, but we were tearing up the house so much that the promoter wanted to change the billing and put the Upsetters as the star of the show because when we got through it would be hard for Little Willie John to get on. But we couldn't do that to him. It was one hell of a moment, though, to hear something like that about our band.

We was in Buffalo, New York, in 1959, getting ready to go onstage with Little Willie John when he called me offstage and asked me to go to the bar with him. He told me to order whatever I wanted, and after I took my first sip he told me he had gotten a telegram that said my father had been killed in Houston. I couldn't believe it. I had to find out what had happened, so I called home and was told that he was killed trying to stop

Grady on stage with Little Willie John in the early '60s. Photo from the Grady Gaines Collection.

a fight between a couple of women and got caught with a punch intended for one of the women in the fight and died afterward. He was only fifty-four years old at the time. I came back home for the funeral, and we took him back to Waskom to be buried. It was just a terrible time for the whole family, but we all came together and dealt with it the best we could.

Meanwhile, though, we continued to be dynamite with women while we was touring with Little Willie John. I remember we was in San Francisco, staying at the Booker T. Washington Hotel, where the band always stayed there, and I had so many women. During the gig, I would spot the ones I wanted to get and slip them my room number. I would line up five, six, seven at a time to have them come to my room. I had two doors to my hotel room; one you'd enter from the outside and another out of the room. After I was through with the woman I had in the room, she would go out the one door while another one would be knocking on the other door. I'd let her in and take care of her, while another one would be waiting downstairs. I'd call down to the desk and tell 'em to send her on up, and I'd do the same thing until I went around the whole bunch.

I never did try to count up how many women I had, but it had to be in the thousands. I did get gonorrhea a couple of times, but I always kept some penicillin with me, so if I got a woman I was suspicious of—if I had any doubts—I'd drop a penicillin pill and kill it before it started. I tried to have a way of playin' that was smart, but those women would be looking so good, pretty, and tender that I couldn't turn it down.

I had every race of woman out there; even had an Indian woman and a Chinese woman, you name it. Pretty much every night I could get as many as I wanted. Me and this cat named Gorgeous George was both dynamite with the women. He would be the emcee on those shows with a bunch of different acts, and while the acts were up there playing, the women would be hollering and pointing at whichever one (band member) they liked, and a lot of 'em would be pointing at my ass. I would just tell 'em to come back around to the side of the stage, and I'd show 'em to the dressing room backstage. That's how I got to talk with 'em.

We were playing this little place in Cincinnati one time with Little Willie John, and this girl was after me throughout the show. Man, she was fine, hairy legs, beautiful. Me and Clifford usually got a room together on the road, but after the show, he already had a woman in there, so the woman said her husband was out of town driving a truck or something, so we went back to her place. Well, she thought he was out of town, but he wasn't. I went in there, and I was gettin' that meat on the couch when her husband came down the stairs while I was on top of her. He had a little gun with him, so I just got up and said, "All I wanna do is just get out," and I backed out the door. When I hit the screen door, I started running and jumped over about three fences. I got scratched on one of them fences, and the scar is still there (on his right hand). He was pointing that gun on me, but he didn't use it.

Driving from gig to gig, there was always the chance for something to go wrong, too. One time we were coming down from New York to play

"GRADY GAINES"
Bandleader and Feature Sax Man
World-Famous Upsetters' Orchestra
P. O. Box 22098, Washington, D. C.

Promotional photo of Grady, circa late '50s/early '60s. Photo from the Grady Gaines Collection.

fifteen or twenty shows in Florida. It was nighttime, and the driver got sleepy, so he pulled over to the side of the road in an area covered with grass and that looked like solid ground. A little while later, somebody woke up, and the truck was easing over into a swamp, so all of the band members had to ease out of the truck one by one on the driver's side or the thing might have slid into that swamp. After we got out, we flagged down a big truck, and he used his chain to pull us out of there.

Another night after a gig in DC, we were driving near Chesapeake Bay, and the driver pulled over so we could sleep in this spot that looked pretty safe, where there was some construction going on. Well, I woke up, and the truck had started rolling on its own toward the bay. Henry Nash was driving but was asleep, so I hit him, and he hit the brakes just before the truck went over the edge into the bay.

Nash usually handled the money for the band, and I remember we were playing five or six days in this one theater, and near the end of the gig we checked up on him and found out he was stealing money, and we wasn't getting paid what we were supposed to get. An argument broke out, and the way things were, if anything went down with Clifford, I'm in it, and if anything went down with me, Clifford would be in it. That's the kind of friends we were. Well, Nash got mad because we caught him in the act, and he pulled his gun out and started cussin' and screamin'. He hit Clifford on the side of the head with the gun, and it went off.

The bullet grazed Clifford's head and knocked him to the floor. Then Nash put the gun on me. I yelled for somebody to call the doctor; then I ran through the bathroom and jumped out of the window. Clifford was lying on the floor, and the rest of the band got help, and the police showed up. The case went to court a few months later, and Clifford could have put Nash under the jail if he wanted to, but he didn't even show up to court. I told him, boy, you sure should've went to court.

While the Upsetters were the primary backing band for Little Willie John, they were also booked to play on lengthy tours that frequently featured multiple entertainers who had hit records on the charts. The Upsetters would play not only behind John but also behind the other acts on the bill during these revue-style shows, which became quite popular in the 1960s.

Charles Sullivan booked a tour with us, Little Willie John, and Sam Cooke that lasted about thirty-five days and went up and down California, then to Arizona, then out to Georgia—all over the place. While we was on tour, Sam's "Twistin' the Night Away" was hittin' like a big dog. When the tour ended, Sam said he wanted this band (now going by the name of Grady Gaines and the Upsetters), so the band talked it over, and we decided to go with Sam, and it became Sam Cooke and the Upsetters. By this time, (drummer) Charles Connor was back in LA, so Emil Russell from Mobile came in as the drummer, and, man, he was a *baaad* drummer, just like Charles.

We toured all over the world with Sam up until he died. He was one of the best people you'd ever want to meet and work for. Between him and Richard, it's a toss-up (on who was the better artist to work for). Before he got killed, he had written some stuff for me to record and was going to record me in Los Angeles on his SAR record label.

We had just finished a tour with Sam and were in Atlanta when Martin Luther King delivered his speech ("I Have a Dream," delivered during the March on Washington, DC, in August 1963). The first thing that came into my mind when I heard his speech was Moses taking his people to the promised land and him telling them that I may not get there with you, but you'll get to the promised land.

When we were touring with Little Willie John in Jamaica, I remember him (King) coming to a gig and sitting up in the crowd (in the balcony). I think he was trying to get away from all the people, so he was sitting in like a box or special corner. He showed up to quite a few of our gigs, but I never did get to meet him. There was a lot of sit-ins and protests going on during that time at department stores and restaurants and places that wouldn't serve black people, and we were traveling around the country in the middle of it. I recall there was a sit-in in Jacksonville (Florida) one time that got real deep. Things didn't change right away

Grady and band backing Smokey Robinson. From left, Grady, Robinson, and acclaimed Motown bassist James Jamerson, circa early '60s. Photo courtesy of the Milton Hopkins Collection.

after the speech, but for a while, I'd say it got a little worse in terms of (white) people treating us bad down South, like not letting us stop to get gas or something to eat.

Of course, that was the same year that President Kennedy got shot. We were in Charlotte (North Carolina) to play a show at the coliseum there and had a day or so off before the show. We were laying up in the hotel drinking and partying when the news flashed on the TV that the president had been shot in Dallas. It was just shocking news because it was like he (Kennedy) was in everybody's house. It seemed like every family felt like he was part of their family—like he was in everybody's heart.

Not too long after that, we played a tour of forty-five one-nighters from one end of the country to the other with Sam Cooke and Jackie Wilson, where Grady Gaines and the Upsetters backed the whole show. One night Sam would open, then Jackie would open the next. That tour also had people like Jerry Butler, Bo Diddley, Solomon Burke, Etta James, Dionne Warwick on some nights, and I think we had B. B. King on a couple of dates. That was a dynamite tour. On some shows, you had to just about pull Sam off the stage; then at another show, you'd have to pull Jackie off the stage. We had a lot of fun on that tour, and I'll never forget it because it was on that tour that we had to have twenty police officers at the Kiel Auditorium (in St. Louis) escort me to the bus after the show because women was trying to grab me and rip my clothes off!

One time when we were in Ohio somewhere with Sam, the tour bus ran over my horn. It was after a gig, and they were loading up, and I walked away from my sax because I was busy concentrating on trying to get in between some girl's legs. The driver didn't see the horn back there and ran over it, and I didn't have a horn for the gig that night. I called H&H Music back in Houston, and they put me a horn on a plane, and I got it in time for the show and didn't miss a stroke.

Milton Hopkins

WHEN WE PLAYED MEMPHIS, it was set to be a segregated show, with whites on one side of the stage and the blacks on the other. Well, you only got one band, and we couldn't face but one direction, so if we faced the whites, the blacks got mad, and if we faced the blacks, the whites got mad. So what we did was turn around and played to the opposite wall, and that worked out. But then out comes Jackie Wilson, and he was tearing up the place singing, doing flips and stuff, and shouting, and people started flooding the stage, and before we knew anything, white people and black people were all over the place dancing and having a hell of a time. The police just gave up. Sam Cooke was all business, but he was always nice to everybody. He was one hell of a performer and really cared about whether his music and arrangements would be played the right way. You couldn't be onstage improvising his stuff. That wouldn't cut it. The only thing I remember that got on his nerves was the fact that we had like twenty-four changes

Milton Hopkins, Sam Cooke, and Clifford Burks in the early '60s. Photo courtesy of the Milton Hopkins Collection.

of clothes, and you'd go onstage with one outfit on, take a break,
and come back with something else on, and that rattled his
chains a little bit.

After that tour in 1964, we wound up back in Atlanta and played three
days at the Peacock on Auburn Avenue. Sam went on vacation, and we
was supposed to meet him in Miami at the Fontainebleau Hotel. Sam
had a meeting scheduled in Los Angeles with some record company
people who wanted to get a controlling interest in him. He had his own
recording company and recorded a lot of people and was making all kinds
of money in the peak of it. He recorded a lot of people, like Johnnie Taylor, who used to stand backstage while we played all the time. He (Sam)
was a very smart man, and I can't say I blame him for not wanting to give
up controlling interest.

Some artists have a jealous streak and don't want to help other artists,
but Sam was just the opposite. He would help any of 'em out. What he
would do was cut a song like "Soothe Me, Baby, Soothe Me" with the
Simms Twins, and it would be a hit. Then he we would go back and
record it over and make it an even bigger hit, so he got paid twice on it.
He did that with just about everybody he was dealing with.

When we played in Los Angeles, we stayed in this one motel that
wasn't in the total ghetto but wasn't that nice either. Sam could stay at
better hotels, but he liked being around the band. He was crazy about
this band, and he would write a whole lot of hit records in the ghetto part
of town because he wanted to be around the band.

But on the road, Sam didn't have time for courtin' and stuff, so he
would just go ahead and get a prostitute. That's the way most of them
cats did it. Well, he got a room at the motel where we'd stayed, and that
same ol' woman (motel manager) shot him. That girl (a prostitute) came
running out like he was raping her, but that ain't Sam. No way. I'd put my
head on the chopping block for that. The way I understood it, he was set
up, but I don't want to go off into all that, though. The band was check-
ing into a hotel in Oklahoma City at seven o'clock in the morning when
we saw on the TV that he'd been killed. Boy, you talk about a hurtin' time.

But we had more dates scheduled, so not too long after Sam was

Promotional poster from early '60s' tour of Jamaica with Sam Cooke. Photo courtesy of the Milton Hopkins Collection.

shot, we toured as L. C. Cooke (Sam's brother) and Grady Gaines and the Upsetters. He could sing good but not as good as Sam. We was still working, but it wasn't like having Sam, and we weren't making much money. L. C. stayed with the band as a singer until I came off the road in the late '60s.

The shooting that claimed Sam Cooke's life took place at the Hacienda Motel on South Figueroa Street in Los Angeles. The manager, Bertha Franklin, told police she had shot Cooke in self-defense because he had attacked her. The coroner's jury ruled the death a case of "justifiable homicide," but to this day the death of Sam Cooke remains shrouded in mystery. Despite the ridiculously busy touring schedule the band experienced while working with Cooke, Grady Gaines, and the Upsetters, at least some of the band managed to get into a recording studio with the prolific singer. As a result, Gaines's horn can be heard on the Cooke classic "Having a Party."

Two years younger than Sam, L. C. Cooke (his name is sometimes spelled without the "e," which was absent in the family's spelling of the name) achieved his greatest success as a "songwriter" for Sam. Due to various recording and music publishing contracts, Sam Cooke credited several songs, including "You Send Me," "That's All I Need to Know," and "Win Your Love for Me" to L. C. to prevent them from falling into the clutches of the publishing executives that Sam battled for control of his music.

L. C. and Sam had sung together as members of the Singing Children, formed by Sam with two of his sisters (Sam was the fifth of ten children born to the Rev. Charles Cook and his wife, Annie May). The two also sang together as members of the Highway QCs, which achieved some modest success in the late '40s. Following Sam's recruitment into the Soul Stirrers in 1951, he and L. C. would sing together no more.

L. C. Cooke, whose powerful voice bore a striking similarity to his famous sibling's, even if it did lack some of Sam's polish and warmth, went on to join the Chicago R&B group the Magnificents, founded by

Johnny Keys, who enjoyed a hit with the song "Up on the Mountain."
Cooke also recorded the single "I Need Your Love" for Chess Records
and in 1960 signed with his brother's newly formed SAR Records label.
But he never was able to sustain any career momentum and faded from
the industry by the late 1960s.

Sam Cooke was inducted into the Rock and Roll Hall of Fame in
1986. In October 2005 Grady was invited to speak on his experiences
touring and recording with Cooke at the tenth annual American Music
Masters program titled "A Change Is Gonna Come: The Life and Music
of Sam Cooke." The weeklong celebration, a coproduction of the Rock
and Roll Hall of Fame and Museum and the College of Arts and Sci-
ences at Case Western Reserve University, was held in Cleveland,
Ohio.[5]

After Sam was killed, we became the main backing band for Universal
Attractions, backing every major artist that was out there. We might play
a few days or weeks with Etta James, Ruth Brown, Bo Diddley, Solomon
Burke, Gladys Knight and the Pips, the Supremes, the Crystals, Patti
Labelle—anybody that was somebody.

And the Upsetters worked hard at being entertaining ourselves.
Back before they had them wireless microphones, which didn't come
around until the late '60s or the '70s, I used to take a 150-foot cord,
stick a mic down the barrel of my horn, and have somebody behind me
pull the cord as I honked and walked the floor. I'd stand on the bar or a
table or a chair—whatever it took to please the crowd. I'd take that long
cord and walk outside on the sidewalk and play, and there would be a
line of people following me outside. Sometimes I'd unplug my horn and
get in a car and ride around the block. I'd come back, and people would
be waiting for me, so I'd plug it back up, go back in the club, and really
tear it up. I did a lot of things to make it come together and make a
living out of music.

We worked our horns pretty hard, too. I didn't ever have a saxophone
break on me onstage, though, but sometimes those little springs (on the
keys) would pop out, but you would just push it back in, and that didn't

happen very often. But before I went onstage I checked everything out, and I'd go on ready. I tried to prepare every time I hit that stage.

One of the people we had a lot of fun with was Bo Diddley. He was a house rocker and had more whites than blacks on his side, but he had some blacks, too. He could hold his own. He was the first one to start getting different sounds out of his guitar with them foot pedals and stuff. He used to make his own amps and get them sounds with tremolos and all that. His amp was this tall (about five feet high and five feet wide). He made all that stuff, and people would take it and modify it and made it what it is today.

Etta James was one of my favorites, too. She was dynamite on that stage. I loved every second of playing behind her. One of my favorite songs of hers was "Tell Mama," and I've played that wedding song of hers ("At Last") so many times. She was wonderful. Just lovely.

This was during the time when promoters would book these revue-type tours that might last forty-five days with sometimes fifteen or twenty acts onstage every night, and my band would play the whole show. Everybody on the show would have a hit record out, and we played all the big theaters like the Apollo in New York, the Howard in Washington, DC, the Regal in Chicago, and the Kiel Auditorium in St. Louis. The Upsetters would open the show and play mostly instrumentals and tear the place up, then each artist would play two or three numbers. The hottest artists might do three or four songs.

By this time, I was living wherever I hung my hat because I was probably on the road 365 days a year and playing maybe 300 nights a year for a stretch. I wasn't married at this time, although I've been married twice, and I had kids all over the place; some I didn't even know I had. My son, Grady Jr., was raised by my mother and his mother's (Faye Shotwell) mother because I was traveling a lot. Later on, I had Derrick and Van by different women. Derrick's a dentist now in Houston, and Van is a police officer in Atlanta. I also have daughters Debra (whose mother is also Faye Shotwell), Wanda, and Tewanda, and they're doing real well. If I'm missing anybody, I apologize, but I was a busy man on that road, and, to be honest, it's hard to put an exact number on how many kids I had. When you're traveling the way we was for as long as we did and to be as popular as we was, you thought there would be no end to having fun. But all of the kids that I had that I know about were taken care of.

We made it back to Houston maybe twice a year at this time, and I know my mama and sisters were worried about us out there on the road. But when we came back home, we had a lot of places to go for dinner before we left the area. We might be playing dates around Houston in Galveston or La Marque or some place. We might have ten or twelve dates and come back home every night. Milton's mama would cook for us. My sister Adrena (Carter) would have dinner for us, then we'd have dinner at my mama's house. Every musician who lived in Houston, we had to have dinner at his mama's house. I'll never forget all of those family-type meals we had, and Adrena—we called her "Tut"—was like a second mother to us and held the family together during this time. When I ran short of money, between her and Uncle Elmore, I had everything I needed.

Wilkie Hartwell, Grady's younger sister

BOY, MY MAMA WOULD COOK these big dinners for 'em. Oh, she had everything: peach cobblers, fried chicken, greens, cakes. Everybody had a good time, and the band members would just eat, eat, eat!

We was playing the chitlin' circuit mostly before rock 'n' roll came out. Once rock 'n' roll came out, things changed because more whites started crossing over with black performers. The only ones I can think of that didn't play the chitlin' circuit was Duke Ellington and maybe Count Basie. But they would play at a white place and had to stay in a chitlin' circuit hotel.

The term "chitlin' circuit" refers to a host of theaters, clubs, diners, and dives throughout the eastern and southern United States that served as safe venues for African American musicians and comedians. The circuit was popular from the 1930s through the mid-1960s.

The chitlin' circuit was for bands that didn't have much crossover (appeal), but it wasn't all bad. What was bad was that you couldn't go over there (white neighborhoods) if you wanted to. When we played the chitlin' circuit, though, there would always be some whites trying to come over to where we was playing. But for our band, once we were out there with Richard, after "Tutti Frutti" came out, we would stay in black hotels, but we was playing in white neighborhoods. Other artists that didn't have much crossover audience played the circuit all the time.

The circuit was cool because you was on your turf, and everybody felt comfortable as long as you stayed in your place. But, see, I was never a troublemaker. So long as you minded yourself and don't get nothing started to get them (white people) to come over there to your side to bother you it was fine. But that was the old days. I'm sure some of that probably still goes on, but it's not as bad as it was. It wasn't right, but that's life. The (chitlin' circuit) crowds was good, but when you had both sides (blacks and whites) coming to your show, the crowds were automatically going to be bigger. We made pretty good money, but once you got that crossover audience, then you knew what real money was.

The chitlin' circuit was where I met Jimi Hendrix. We were on some of those long tours together when he was Gorgeous George's (born Theophilus Odell George) guitar player. We rode on the buses together and talked a lot about stuff musicians talk about—like girls and the next gig. He was a regular guy, but he was one of them trick-type guitar players and never was a heck of a singer. But he wound up being a hell of a cat on the other side of the fence (with white audiences).

(Producer) Mr. Wiggles (born Alexander Randolph) had a record company in the '60s (Sound of Soul), and I remember recording a song called "KP Cabbage and Greens" that supposedly had Jimi on guitar, but the guitar player could have been Melvin Sparks, who was in our band for a while. I think Mr. Wiggles went back and put Jimi on the track because I don't remember recording with Jimi.

An instrumental titled "Cabbage Greens" was released in 1965 on Mr. Wiggles's Sound of Soul Records (SS 105B) and credits "The

World Famous Upsetters" as the artist, with Gaines listed as the song-writer. Many Jimi Hendrix researchers insist that the guitar part on the song was not played by Hendrix because the playing is not in the same style Hendrix was playing in the midsixties. Several Hendrix archivists believe the lead part was indeed played by Melvin Sparks, the Houston-born guitarist who died in 2011 at age sixty-four.[6]

I didn't know about any of the drugs people said Jimi was doing back then. Actually, we didn't have too much trouble with drugs or alcohol in the Upsetters. I did keep me a half pint of whiskey or something in my coat pocket, though, just to keep my spirits up. I got that from Cab Calloway. Back when I was still in high school, he had heard about the Blues Ramblers and actually came to my house one day to try to get me to join his band. I remember he just came walking down the street. He talked to my mama about me going on the road with him, but she thought I was too young for that at the time. But I do remember him having that flask in his coat, so I just did the same thing and always had me one in my makeup bag.

Some of the bands we played behind were into the drugs. Hank Ballard and the Midnighters did a lot of stuff on a tour we did with them. But drugs like marijuana and stuff, I stayed a distance from it. I didn't want to go to jail. I'd never been to jail and didn't want to go. It was people around us that were doing that stuff and I guess some people in our band, too, but I didn't hang out with none of that.

One thing that helped make us so popular was the way we looked and played onstage. We worked hard at being exciting for the audience wherever we played. We was always movin' and dancin' and always dressed the part. I designed just about every outfit we wore onstage for a long time. If I didn't design it, I would go and pick 'em out at the tailor's shop and get the band to come check 'em out. I even designed some of the stuff Little Richard wore in the early days. I gave him ideas for some things like slacks suits and different little things, but Richard had a lot of good ideas about what he wanted to wear. Being raised in the Fifth Ward, I knew this guy named Johnny Burton at Caldwell Tailors. Johnny was younger than Mr. Caldwell (shop owner Booker T. Caldwell) and a little bit older than me, so he was right there with me on anything I came up with.

Anything I wore, it would have to be different. That was just my way of thinking. Even if I just bought a suit in a store, that suit would be different. I would take a design and draw it on a piece of paper and sit down and visualize it. Sometimes I might take a little from things in a magazine, like I might take a collar here or something else there and put it all together and get a Grady Gaines outfit.

When we went into the Apollo Theater for the first time with Little Willie John, I designed fifteen changes of uniform. We played the Apollo for a week. We'd go in on Friday and play three shows a day. On Saturday we'd play a midnight show, which meant we played four shows. We'd play Friday through Thursday, and we wouldn't wear the same thing until that Tuesday night. Every one of 'em would be eye-catching.

I would design everything myself, and if the cats in the band didn't want to pay for them, I might pay for 'em myself. Sometimes they might say I had them looking kinda gay, but all I wanted to do was get the crowd with all the colors and designs so when we came out of the show we be done tore that show up.

Johnny Burton made most of them, but Duke's Men's Shop on Travis Street (in Houston) used to make a lot of things for me, too. I recall when people used to wear these shirts with long rabbit-ear collars that I designed that got real popular; then them slacks suits, same thing. I designed that. I drew it up, and Duke's Men's Shop made it. All of the groups that would come to town and stay at the Club Matinee would be wearing them shirts with long collars. Everybody started making those shirts, and then I started seeing them in other stores across town. When artists came through, they would be wearing them, then somebody else would see 'em and pick up on it, so it migrated across the country. I've always been creative, and I didn't want to look like nobody else. I could've been rich if I had copyrighted all the designs I made, but I didn't know anything about marketing. I wanted to be different, but not so different that I was totally out of the pocket.

THE UPSETTERS ORCHESTRA

Promotional photo of the Upsetters Orchestra in the early '60s. From left, Milton Hopkins, Clifford Burks, Emil Russell, Grady, Larry Lanier, O. C. "Bassie" Robertson. Photo courtesy of the Milton Hopkins Collection.

Booker T. Caldwell opened his haberdashery in Houston in 1951, and it became the go-to shop for a wide range of black leaders, athletes, and entertainers. The store was originally located on Lyons Avenue in the Fifth Ward near the Club Matinee, but Caldwell later moved it into the Third Ward building that had housed the famous Eldorado Ballroom. It was located down the street from the Crystal Hotel, cited by many as the finest hotel for blacks in the city at the time, which helped to bring many potential customers into the shop.

In his book *Down in Houston: Bayou City Blues*, author Roger Wood writes that Peacock Records impresario Don Robey owned a nearby barbershop and was a regular customer. Robey referred countless artists to Caldwell Tailors to get outfitted in the hippest stage wardrobe offerings. Tour buses full of musicians staying at the hotel or playing at the Club Matinee would often pull up in front of the shop. Some of the artists who benefited from Caldwell's keen sense of style, according to Wood, included Clarence "Gatemouth" Brown, Buddy Ace, Charles Brown, Texas Johnny Brown, Ray Charles, Clifton Chenier, Johnny Copeland, Clarence Green, Lightnin' Hopkins, B. B. King, Pete Mayes, Jimmy "T-99" Nelson, Calvin Owens, and Jimmy Reed. The shop closed in 2004 at its final location on Elgin in the Third Ward. Caldwell, whose son is noted Houston minister Kirbyjon Caldwell, pastor of the Windsor Village United Methodist Church, passed away in 2011 at the age of eighty-eight. According to his obituary in the *Houston Chronicle*, Caldwell in 1999 earned the Heritage Award from the Houston Citizens Chamber of Commerce in recognition of his lifetime achievement in business.[7]

The other thing that separated us from a lot of bands then was our showmanship. We worked hard at being exciting—moving around and dancin' onstage. Today they got so much showmanship on TV, but we didn't have nothing like that when I came along. You couldn't see it and copy from what somebody else did; you had to develop it yourself with your imagination. I did get some of our onstage stuff from Illinois Jacquet. They used to have these little jukeboxes where you'd put in fifty cents and you could see them (Jacquet, Louis Jordan, and other popular entertainers) play their tunes (short film clips known as "soundies"). I liked the way they did things, the way they played—the whole deal. Showmanship-wise, they was something else. But I didn't do their stuff. I always tried things on my own and tried to be different.

But it's all there today. If somebody can't get no showmanship today, I don't understand it. By me traveling and playing behind so many differ-ent artists—playing behind some of the hottest acts in the country—we got a chance to see a lot of different ones, so we took whatever we could and made it our own and learned through experience.

I know for a fact that Michael Jackson's daddy (Joe Jackson) used to bring the Jackson 5 by the Apollo to watch us onstage. He was taking them around to theaters because he was trying to get them out there and let them see the best acts out there.

Back in the '60s, booking agencies divided up the country and booked you into certain areas, and they all had their territories. We worked mainly with Universal Attractions on West Fifty-Seventh Street in New York. It was owned by Ben Bart, and he would book us all around the New York area, but he could lease us out to any other agency that he wanted. Teddy Powers owned another agency out of New Jersey, so they (Universal and Powers) handled the East Coast all the way down to Washington, DC, and sometimes into Richmond (Virginia). You had Henry Wayne and B. B. Beamon in Atlanta, who handled all of Georgia, Tennessee, and Florida. Then you had another promoter who would pick up in Texas. Howard Lewis was the promoter in Dallas, and even though Texas is a big state, he practically handled the whole thing. Charles Sullivan booked everything in Arizona, California, and all the way up and down the West Coast and even some parts of Canada.

Being as popular and as busy as we was then, traveling was just a way of life, but it wasn't always easy. To be traveling and being black out there wasn't like it is now. You was in trouble sometimes from so many differ-ent things and people out to do you wrong, like picking on you or harass-ing you. A place like Conroe, Texas (just north of Houston), was one of the worst towns you could go through. It was hard to go through without getting a ticket for a long time. But any small town, and sometimes big towns, could be a problem. Most of the time in a small town they would take you to a judge, and they could do whatever they want with you. Alabama, Georgia, Mississippi, Texas—anywhere in the South could be trouble, but there wasn't any one particular place that was worse than others. For a long time, Mississippi was a tough one, and in Alabama, it depended on how lucky you were to get through that state.

But touring all over the world is where we earned our reputation. Before I left Houston, I was playing in the number-one band in town (Blues Ramblers), and we kept that going even though the musicians would change. But you have to fit the music to whatever musicians you're playing with. If you go from playing with Little Richard to all of a sudden playing with Little Willie John, that's a big difference, so you gotta change. I was always able to do that because I had musicians who were able to do it and do a good job of it.

I remember going into the Stax Records studio (in Memphis) one time, and we recorded a bunch of stuff that was gonna be put on an album, but I never heard anything about it until I heard it come out with different people playing it, and it was something like what we had done in the studio. So I can't say for sure, but what people call the "Memphis sound" owes something to us, I believe.

We recorded an album out in LA for (producer/promoter) H. B. Barnum where we cut a thing called "Let's Get a Thing Going On" and four other sides, but I never heard it. Bands was always trying to get that sound we had with the baritone (sax), two tenors, guitar, and bass. Milton was the backbone of the rhythm section and would carry the whole rhythm without the piano a lot of times. A lot of times we went to Los Angeles, and somebody else be done called themselves the California Upsetters or something. They were playing "Let's Get a Thing Going On." So there were other groups of Upsetters doing the same thing—using the name that we worked so hard to build.

Milton Hopkins

I GOT A COPY of that album we cut with Barnum on cassette years later. Barnum was running up and down the West Coast with it, putting groups together and calling them the Upsetters. We didn't know Barnum had released it, but we were on the other side of the country and couldn't do much about it. I got posters on the wall in my music room at home that somebody sent me from Washington, DC, that say, "The Upsetters. The New Orleans Connection." That really took some balls.

What helped make the Upsetters so powerful was that we could play just about any style of music, from blues to R&B to jazz. You have to take a look at the people in the crowd and play what they want. Even now I'm a good crowd reader. If I'm playing for a crowd and I see a certain age range, I test 'em with something, and if whatever I test 'em with don't work, I know to go somewhere else until I get 'em. I watch the dance floor, and I've never had no problem putting people on the dance floor wherever I go. I've always tried to play according to where I am and the people I'm playing for, and that way I usually come out all right. It just comes with experience. But back then, by the midsixties, you could see things was changing for bands like us, and no matter how much experience you had, it couldn't make up for them big changes that was comin' down the pike in the music business.

CHAPTER 9

Exit Stage Left

When disco came in in the late '60s and early '70s, it kind of curbed everything we was doing. Bands wasn't working, and if you got a band and you're not working, you gonna have to do something. Some of my band members went with other bands, but they weren't working much, either, so we all had to try to make money some kinda way, and it put me in a real bind where I had to get me a job. I don't think I'd ever worked before other than throwing newspapers. But I always said if it ever comes a time when the music don't be right and I'm not making money, I'm gonna do something that I like to do, so I got off the road and came back to Houston to regroup.

A contributing factor in the demise of the performing blues and R&B music scene in the mid- to late sixties and early seventies was that blacks, who had long composed the lion's share of the audience, had begun to abandon blues and, to an extent, R&B music. Sociologists point to the role that increasing desegregation played in changing many of the customs that blacks had embraced. As they were able to move about more freely and as their educational and occupational opportunities increased, many blacks began to long for more sophisticated music and sounds that weren't born on the plantation or the Mississippi delta. As a result, many nightclubs and other music venues that had been dedicated to blues and R&B began closing their doors. Blues artists such as B. B. King and Buddy Guy have spoken openly about struggling to maintain their careers in the face of dwindling opportunities in the late '60s and early '70s.

It wasn't until the mid- to late seventies, when an increasing number of young white fans, hungry for music with depth and soul, gained an appreciation for classic blues and helped to revive the careers of many older blues performers. In fact, many blues players who had struggled to eke out a living playing small dives on the chitlin' circuit did not begin making real money playing music until the early 1980s, when whites began embracing blues and R&B music. Today, whites, for the most part, make up the majority of fans who attend live blues shows by the handful of black headliners still touring, like King, Guy, and Robert Cray.

B. B. King was a big hit with black folks for years, just like other blues guys like Albert Collins, Buddy Guy, and Joe "Guitar" Hughes, but as time passed, the Negroes put it away and didn't want to have much to do with it anymore, unless they were somebody who came up in that time that still liked the blues. But when Negroes dropped it, the whites picked it up, and they picked it up and took it to another level to get to a wider audience. They started playing the blues, and, in my opinion, they start trying to play the way black boys played it, but by them being white, their feelings be different, and it came out like the way Stevie Ray Vaughan and cats like that be playing. What they playing is something else; it's a hell of a thing. He's (Vaughan) actually creating the real blues into another part of the blues, which is still good blues in my opinion. Like me when I started playing, I was trying to play like Louis Jordan and Gene Ammons, but it come out a different way. That's the way most of the white guys started, by trying to play it like black guys, but when it come out, it come out their way.

The black audience had put it (blues) to the side, but blues was new to the white crowd, and they were more accepting because it's a new thing to them. The majority of the white crowd had never heard the blues before a white person started playing it.

With the Upsetters breaking up, I was trying anything I could do to get jobs. I went to Mexico with Little Richard after he called me to play some dates with him there. He was calling the band Little Richard and the Crown Jewels, so I told him I was gonna use that name, too, and when I got back to Houston, I started Grady Gaines and the Crown Jewels. I used a variety of musicians in the Crown Jewels, but the main ones were Teddy Reynolds (piano) and Johnny Perry (drums), Floyd Arceneaux (trumpet), Michael Dogan (bass), John Andrews (guitar), and Henry Moore was the singer. He could sing just like Johnnie Taylor.

Even though he had ceased touring on a national level and was living in Houston, by the mid-1960s, Grady still maintained an occasionally busy schedule that consisted of playing primarily small clubs in the Houston area, the Dallas–Fort Worth Metroplex, and various cities in Texas, including Beaumont, Baytown, and San Antonio, as well as Louisiana. Playing at Southeast Texas clubs like the G&M Pleasure Spot in La Marque, the Drag Kitchen in Orange, Shorty's Place in Beaumont, the Blue Room in Baytown, Club Astronaut in Bay City, and McDaniel's Lounge, the Silver Slipper, and Vivian's Lounge in Houston's Fifth Ward was a hardscrabble life and a world away from the Apollo or Howard theaters and the other large and prestigious venues that he had grown accustomed to playing as a member of the Upsetters. His bands backed a variety of artists, including Johnnie Taylor, Lowell Fulson, Eddie Floyd, Joe "Guitar" Hughes, Joe Hinton, Johnny Copeland, Buddy Ace, and Joe Medwick. Concert posters from the period indicate that in addition to the Crown Jewels, Gaines performed under names such as "Grady Gaines and His Orchestra," "Grady Gaines and His All Stars," "Pretty Grady Gaines," and simply as "Grady Gaines."

In 1966, Grady's band was playing a gig at Houston's Club Ebony, backing blues guitarist Albert Collins, when the guitarist introduced Gaines to a twenty-two-year-old white Houston guitar player named John Andrews, who had befriended Collins a couple of years earlier. Andrews, who now owns Texas Ceiling Fans in Austin, went on to become a member of the California blues-rock outfit led by singer Tracy Nelson, called Mother Earth, and once jammed with Jimi Hendrix when the would-be superstar was playing in a band called Jimmy James and the Blue Flames.

John Andrews, guitarist, 1966–1968

I KNEW ALBERT COLLINS because he had played at my senior prom (Andrews graduated from Houston's Spring Branch High School) at Memorial Country Club, and we had a party in our backyard afterward, where Albert and his band played. When he took a break that night at Club Ebony, he wanted to introduce me to Grady. Grady asked me what I did, and I told him I played guitar, so he said I should get up (onstage) and play with his band. Grady's guitar player was leaving to go to San Francisco, and Grady offered me the gig in his band the next day.

It was early spring of 1966 when I played my first gig with Grady. It was on a Sunday night at the Drag Kitchen in Orange. It was the place where Gatemouth Brown had gotten his start way back in the '40s. I was the only white guy in the band, and as far as I know, Grady's band was the first integrated band in Houston. We got to the club around six o'clock in the evening in Grady's black Chrysler station wagon that we traveled in, and the owner came out and said to Grady, "I don't believe we're gonna have much of a crowd tonight." Grady said, "How come?" and the man said, "Well, Saturday night we had a ruckus here, and three people got shot and killed!" I said to myself, "Man, what did I get myself into?" Some of these places we played were really rough, with shootings and stuff. We used to play at Shorty's Place on the main drag in Beaumont, and it was really rough. It was an old theater, so the stage was high off the floor, and they had chicken wire in front of the stage, and people would throw beer bottles at the stage if they didn't like the band. Of course, they loved Grady.

We would play the Drag Kitchen on Fridays and Shorty's on Saturday, and we played the Blue Room in Baytown a lot. That place was so rough the guys in the band called it "Tombstone Territory" because there were so many shootings. I remember we were doing three dates with Lowell Fulson, one in Houston and three at the Club Astronaut in Bay City. It was a big club, held about five hundred people. Lowell's brother, Robert, a big guy who must have weighed about three hundred pounds, was the promoter and took the money at the door. He threw some drunk guy out of the club, but he went out and got his .22 rifle and shot Robert at point-blank range. We were up onstage getting ready to bring Lowell on, and all of a sudden everybody started running. Our bass player said, "Get off the stage. I'll meet you in the men's room. Somebody's been shot!"

Robert was on the floor with his hands over his chest and told me, "I been shot!" Blood was everywhere, and they took him to the hospital. He wound up being OK and lived through it, but the police came and never did find the guy who shot him. We went on with the show and left the club around two thirty in the morning. When Grady went out to the car to drive off, the guy (gunman) was hiding under his car. Well, the police station was about two blocks away, and Grady drove over there and told them the guy had been hiding under his car. I guess they went down there and arrested him, but we didn't wait around to hear.

Another time we were playing at the G&M Pleasure Spot in La Marque, and it was one of the best clubs to play at then. We were backing up Johnnie Taylor, and my girlfriend was with me. We had met Johnnie in Memphis at the Stax (Records) Studios. We were talking in the dressing room, and it was time to hit (go onstage). Johnnie was holding a rolled-up towel and told my girlfriend to follow him to the stage, and when we bring him on, he'd give her the towel to take back to his dressing room. We started the show and brought Johnnie on, and he gave the towel to my girlfriend. When she got back to his dressing room, she unwrapped the towel, and a .38 pistol fell out and fired on the floor.

We played a few gigs as the Crown Jewels before I ran into Roy Crane, who was the manager for Johnnie Taylor (he also managed Sam Cooke for a period in the '60s). Crane was dropping somebody off at the airport, and I had got a job working as a security guard at the gate in front of the air traffic control center (at Houston's Intercontinental Airport), and he talked to me about playing with Johnnie Taylor. I told him right there that I would, so I quit my job and went on the road with Johnnie for about four or five months.

We was going from Atlanta to Oklahoma City with Johnnie Taylor when we heard that Martin Luther King had been shot (in 1968). We didn't have to cancel any shows, but there was a lot of riots and stuff going on around the country. There was a bad riot in Jacksonville (Florida), but we missed it. We heard about it beforehand and didn't go in there. But we were again in the middle of all this stuff that hit the fan then around people trying to bring progress to this country and trying to get rights that everybody needed and was trying to get.

A little while later Johnnie came through Houston and told me to pick out a PA system to buy. There was this Shure system with stand-up cabinets that he wanted, so I got it, and he made me in charge of everything, including getting things set up for gigs. The last date of the tour was in Atlanta on a Friday or Saturday night, and Johnnie hadn't paid the band off yet before he went back to Dallas. He left me with the band not being paid, and even though it wasn't my band—I was the bandleader—I got money from my own savings account to pay the band off. Me and Preston Thomas, the alto sax player, brought all of the equipment back to my house.

There was a house that belonged to my mama on the lot next door to my house, so we locked all the equipment up in there. Johnnie sent people down here to pick it up, but I told them they couldn't get the stuff unless he paid me for the band money. He had the money, but that was just Johnnie Taylor. Johnnie said he wasn't going to pay me, but I had talked to some lawyers, and I told him he couldn't get the equipment by law unless he paid me, so he sent the money, and I got the equipment out for him. But after that, we had problems with money in the band, so I quit and came back to Houston.

John Andrews

I NEVER HAD NO PROBLEMS being the only white guy in the band. Nobody ever bothered me because I was just part of the band, and everybody accepted it. Grady was like a big brother to me and looked out for me. But one night we were playing at Vivian's Lounge in the Fifth Ward, and some younger kids I knew who had a band and knew who the Upsetters were came to hear us play. They were drinking beer when the vice squad came in and arrested them for being underage. After the band break, I told Grady "I'm gonna go over there and talk to the vice squad officer and get his badge number for the way they roughed up those kids." Grady told me to stay away from it and don't fool with the cops because I was just gonna get myself in trouble. Well, I went over there and said, "I want your badge number because I'm gonna report you." The cop slammed me on the ground, threw me in the (police) car, and took me down to the Harris County jail, and threw me in the drunk tank even though I hadn't had anything to drink. It was about 3 a.m. when the jailer said, "Mr. Andrews. Come out here. Somebody's bailing you out." I got out there, and it was Grady who had gotten the money, and he took me home.

There was one time when I was pretty uncomfortable, and Grady was worried about me, too. We were playing at a victory party for Muhammad Ali at the Black Muslim temple in the Third Ward. Ali had won a big fight in New York and was living in Houston at the time and was flying back. He got there around five o'clock in the afternoon.

There were three or four black Muslim teachers in their black suits, white shirts, and black ties welcoming the band onstage, saying something like, "Good evening sir. Glad to have you here." When they got to me, I put my hand out, and they didn't say anything and wouldn't shake my hand. We started playing, and Grady had worked it out so when Ali got there, he would get a cue from the back of the club, and we would break into a shuffle once he got there. Ali comes in with a couple of bouncers and walks onstage. We start doing the "Ali Shuffle," and all of a sudden Ali turned around and saw me and looked at Grady, who told him, "He cool, man." I figure I must have been the only white musician to ever play there, and Grady was worried about me getting out of there, so I rode with him, and he dropped me off at my car that was parked a little ways away.

We played a New Year's Eve gig at the G&M Pleasure Spot with Joe Hinton, and I had this old Renault. I got about four or five miles from La Marque, and the car threw a rod. I grabbed my guitar and walked a couple of miles and found a redneck beer joint and went inside to use the phone. I called the G&M and got Grady on the phone. We were fixing to hit, and I told Grady I'm in here with these rednecks, and Grady said, "I'll pick you up." Grady comes in with his skintight stage suit on, and, man, they looked at him . . . They didn't say nothing, though, and I picked up my guitar and left.

John Andrews was a great addition to the band and a hell of a guitar player. I'm pretty confident saying that we were the first all-black band in Houston to hire a white musician. I can remember when we'd be playing at Vivian's Lounge, and he would be playing so hard, playing with his teeth and so forth, and sometimes his teeth would be bleeding all over the place. He'd look at me and say, "Grady, that's soul blood."

We started doing shows around this time with the Grady Gaines Go-Go Girls, which were two girls who went by the name the Ghetto Sisters, who wore them short-shorts and would dance while the band was playing. We was also the house band at the Club Ebony for a while. We'd open up the show, then the main band did their show. My son Derrick's mother, Jean Castleberry, always followed the band and carried a crowd of nothing but ladies with her. I had a ten-piece band then, and each member had a girlfriend who would bring their friends to our gigs, so everywhere we played, we had a packed house.

Joe Tex called me about this time because he'd heard that I was free. I had known Joe Tex almost all of his life because he had played talent shows at the Club Matinee put on by a DJ named Trommy King, so I told him I was ready to work. I met Joe in Detroit, and the first club we played was the 20 Grand. Then we toured all over New York, the Carolinas, then out to California, and it was real good. He had a fifteen- to sixteen-piece band at the time, and that big band hit me just right, but I decided I didn't want to do it (tour with Tex) anymore because the money wasn't good enough. What money we made we had to put right back into the band for hotels and food, so I wasn't able to bring no money home, plus I was losing all my contacts around Houston, and it felt like I was spinning my wheels. I couldn't be out there spinning my wheels and wind up losing my house. I've always been a person that looks ahead for things that could happen, and I knew I gotta have a place to stay if I ever came off the road for good. I left Joe Tex while we were in Los Angeles and came back to Houston. That's when I left the road for good.

The raspy-voiced Joe Tex (born Joseph Arrington in 1933 in Rogers, Texas) was an influential, if underappreciated, soul singer in the '60s and '70s. Equally adept at ballads and bawdy, raucous soul tunes drenched in hyperbole, Tex gained some notoriety, if not big sales, with funky and playful songs such as "One Monkey Don't Stop No Show" in 1965 and "Skinny Legs and All" in 1967. "I Gotcha" (1972) proved to be a chart success, reaching number two on the pop chart and number one on the R&B chart after selling some three million copies. "Ain't Gonna Bump No More (with No Big Fat Woman)," with its disco-inflected groove, reached the top ten on the R&B chart and number twelve on the pop chart in 1977. Tex died of a heart attack in 1982 at age 49.[1]

John Andrews

GRADY GOT THE CALL from Joe Tex in January of '68 and said Joe wanted him to come to Memphis to do some recording at American Studios and go on the road with him. Grady left, and (alto sax player) Preston Thomas took over the band, but it just wasn't the same at all. If Grady hadn't left, I probably would've stayed in the band, but I learned so much from him. I learned professionalism from Grady: how to run a band and a show and how to be on time for a gig and how to dress onstage. I learned how to "play in the pocket," and Grady always told me that less is more and don't try to show off with a bunch of solos. He said it's more important to play what you feel and play in the pocket. And I learned how to read chord charts, so when I left to go to Los Angeles, I was a seasoned guitar player.

When I first came off the road and went back to Houston, I stayed at the house my mama owned right next to the house I live in now. My mama was a hell of a cook and had worked for a white lady that owned a hamburger stand, so she was able to buy the little house. It was torn down years ago, but I still own the lot. I stayed in that little house with my mama for a little while until I got married to Eunice Alvis. I'd met her when I was on the road doing a big show near Louisville, Kentucky. I think she was from a town called Earlington (Kentucky).

I had met her after the gig and liked her a whole lot. She was real pretty. I took her to a party at a hotel for Muhammad Ali, who was still Cassius Clay at the time. We had a lot of fun at that party, and he (Ali) talked a lot of crazy shit about how pretty he is. I'd say, "Boy, you're crazy." After the party me and her went back to my room and got real tight. I never lost contact with her and wound up marrying her. She told me that she had had a daughter, but it wasn't my girl. But that girl still looks at me like her father because I was the only one there for her. I took her shopping and whatever else fathers do. Her name is Angela Mills, and she's married now.

Me and Eunice were married for about three or four years, but it (the marriage) didn't last because I could see some things that I didn't want to see that I didn't talk about. She said I was drinking too much, but I said I ain't gonna quit. That wasn't the total reason; there was more to it than that. Anyway, she left, and I had bought all kinds of furniture and stuff, and all the bills were left on me, and I didn't know how I was going to come out of that.

I had been married in the '60s to a girl named Marilyn from Fort Worth. I had met her at a show in Dallas back when I was on the road full time. I took a day off to get married in Fort Worth and had twenty cars follow me from Houston to Fort Worth because nobody expected me to be getting married with all the girls I had, so people knew it wasn't my style. She was a schoolteacher, and we got along pretty good, but we broke up after a little while. It wasn't about drinking; it was about other stuff that I don't want to talk about. We had an apartment over on Lockwood, but I wasn't in town much, and this is when everywhere I went there were women pulling on me, and some of them looked so good that you can't refuse.

I was able to get a job through a good friend who stuck with me through the whole hardship when I wasn't playing much. His name was Elgin Lewis, and he wrote for the *Houston Forward Times* (a newspaper focused on Houston's black community). He passed away a while back, but we were as close as any brothers. He felt that way about me, and I felt that way about him. He'd come to my house and act like he was at home. He'd go in the refrigerator and get himself something to eat or drink, or he'd go in there (back bedroom of Grady's home) and lay down in the bed—whatever he wanted.

Elgin kept me in the *Forward Times* and tried to make me as popular as possible. He always had things to say (in the paper) to keep me out there with the public, and he had connections with all kinds of people like the people at Colt 45 Malt Liquor. I did advertisements, posters, commercials, whatever I could do, and it helped to keep my name out there. We spent every Sunday at my place or his trying to figure out how to get my name out there. I'm grateful to him to this day for what he did, but he didn't just stop at doing that in the paper or getting me advertisements. He got me a job, too.

He had started working at the Holiday Inn at the airport (now called George Bush Intercontinental Airport Houston) and called for me to come out there one day, and he took me directly to the manager. Elgin got me hired, and I started working as a bellman on the 11 p.m. to 7 a.m. midnight shift. I started making money and started to get my bills and house note paid, which is one of the ways I saved the house I'm living in now.

I put my horn away in the attic, and it stayed there for several years. I worked my way from being a bellman and started working the day shift as the assistant transportation manager (a job that primarily entailed transporting hotel guests to and from the airport via van). I was making good money with some good tips. I eventually became the transportation manager at the Sheraton Hotel and was a skycap for Delta Airlines. I enjoyed working at the hotels and the airport because I lived around 'em for years, and I liked dealing with people.

It wasn't real easy coming off the road, though. Anytime you stay on the road for twenty years without touching home to stay and you come back, it's almost like you're a new person in town as far as gigs go. So you have to rebuild your whole catalog and band, and there were some difficult days there.

Milton Hopkins

I HAD LEFT THE UPSETTERS in the early '70s after a girl I met in San Francisco got pregnant and we got married, so I hadn't seen Grady in a few years. Grady had been having some type of problem. He was working a day job like me and was drinking a lot. I think for a time he had given up, but in the meantime, my band, the Untouchables, was going strong, and I had heard that Grady had quit the business, so I went to his house to talk to him and tell him to clean up his horn and start playing again.

People say I had a drinking problem, but I say if I *hadn't* drank I probably wouldn't be here now. I'd have been crazy from worrying about all the different things happening to me in my life and adjusting myself to the changes happening to me. When things got tough around me, I'd take me a drink. But I'm gonna stay around the house and not be out there acting a fool. After I got my band back together, people would tell me, "I don't know how you do this." I'd say, "Look, I've got a twelve- or thirteen-piece band, and I got that many personalities, and not all of them are pleasurable to deal with." If I didn't have something to help me cope with the personalities that are so against me . . . I hadn't done a thing; nothing but good to them. If they (band members) needed money, I'd give it to 'em; whatever they'd ask of me I'd try to do it. Some people say I'm too easy, but that's just my nature. This is what brought on the drinking. I ain't telling nobody to do this, but it worked for me and kept me going—gave me strength to go on. I didn't do nothing to hurt nobody, and I didn't miss no jobs, and I kept all the musicians together when people was steady wanting them back (in bands they had previously played in), and later on we was playing so many dates that we couldn't play 'em all.

One thing I did then that was pretty out there was I came up with the "Sheik of Soul" thing. This was when soul music was really hot in the '70s, and I was just trying to come up with ways to get my name out there. I designed this white robe and a suit that looked Arabian or something. I had another one in brown with rhinestones. I wore it one time on the plane from Houston to LA, and people thought I was Arabian, but it worked for a long time and got me some work.

A really nice gig I took was to back up T-Bone Walker on his last Houston dates. It must have been early in 1975, and he had called me to put a band together because he was coming to town to play for a week at a place called La Bastille in Market Square (in downtown Houston). It went real well, but after he played those dates, he went back to LA and died a few months later.

One good thing about coming off the road is that me and Grady Jr. got to know each other. Over the years, me and Grady Jr. were tight, but we wasn't tight, you know, because he thought I should be what he wanted me to be, and I'm not about to change my ways. My momma raised him when I was on the road, and she got married again, to Jack Douglas, when Grady was in college. That's how he got the name Grady Douglas. A lot of times he used the name Grady Gaines Jr., and that's what he uses now when he performs, but on contracts and stuff it's Grady Douglas.

He thought I should act the way he thought I should, and he couldn't understand me being with so many women and couldn't understand me drinking. He couldn't understand a whole lot of things, but I wasn't about to change, no way. He put his first wife through that sanctimonious stuff, and she left him cold, so things started happening to him that let him know what real life is about. It ain't what you thought it was. If you ain't experienced no real life, how you going to be trying to tell somebody who's been all over the world and did some of everything to be done in the real world how to act? But that's in the past. We real tight now.

Grady Gaines Jr. and Grady in the early '90s. Photo from the Grady Gaines Collection.

Grady Gaines Jr. is an accomplished musician in his own right, but music has always been secondary to his career in pharmacy. A graduate of the highly respected pharmacy program at Houston's Texas Southern University, Gaines, sixty-one, whose mother is Faye Shotwell, now works as a research pharmacist for Harris Health (formerly the Harris County Hospital District) in Houston. Because Grady Sr. was constantly on the road during his childhood and his mother was living the "fast life" on Houston's streets, Grady Jr. was raised primarily

by his father's mother (Ethel Mae Harris Gaines) and was officially
adopted by her when he was seven. After receiving a saxophone as a
gift from his father when he was around twelve or thirteen, Grady Jr.
progressed quickly on the instrument and was first-chair saxophone
in the prestigious Kashmere Stage Band at Houston's Kashmere High
School. A deeply religious man who has a degree in biblical counsel-
ing from the College of Biblical Studies in Houston, Gaines Jr. played
in several bands, including the Soul Senders, and currently performs
as a duo with keyboardist James Dreeson, with a jazz-centered group
called Quiet Storm, and as a solo performer. Gaines also frequently performs with the Upsetters. A father of five, ranging in age from sixteen to
twenty-nine, Grady Gaines Jr. resides in the Houston area.

Grady Gaines Jr.

I NEVER SAW HIM (Grady Sr.) because he was on the road constantly, but I knew he was out there somewhere. When I was a
kid, I'd see him maybe three or four times a year when he came
to town to visit his mother. Being that young, I didn't know he
was well known or played with famous people; I was just a little
kid trying to make it from day to day. One memory that stands
out was he had a suit made for me when he was in town once. It
was a tailor-made suit that I think came from Caldwell Tailors.
Then he gave me a saxophone when I was in sixth or seventh
grade, and I started messing around with that. He came off the
road in my later years in high school, and I got to spend some
time with him and got to know him. When I was in college, I
stayed with him for a short period of time, and I got to talk to
him and know him a little better and began to put some things
together. I always went to church every Sunday and felt that God
touched her (his grandmother) to take me in after she had raised
all of those people, so I knew my situation was nothing but a gift
from God. I tried to stay out of trouble and didn't drink or smoke
and tried to stay close to God. He helped me see things about

him (Grady Sr.) that I didn't realize. After I got past being hurt or disappointed, it was all good. I flipped the script and became thankful and appreciative and realized he was a very nice person, and if not for him, I wouldn't be here.

My grandmother always wanted me and my father to have a father-son relationship, but it couldn't be like that on a certain level because he was not there, and she (grandmother) was there for everything. So today, me and Grady are close, but not close in the way it would be if you are there with somebody day after day.

Grady with granddaughters Jada Douglas Gaines and Jalaina Douglas Gaines, Grady Jr.'s daughters. Photo from the Grady Gaines Collection.

"Ain't Nothin' for a Stepper"

In the mideighties Milton Hopkins had the gig as the house band at Etta's Lounge (in Houston). I played with him one night, and he said, "Grady, with all that horn you blowin' tonight, you need to start blowing that horn again." So I played there a few nights and at a few other places, and I thought as long as I'm doing this, I might as well get my own band. Milton left the Etta's gig, and I took it over and stayed there playing Sunday nights for about twenty years.

From the outside, Etta's Lounge, located in Houston's Fifth Ward, doesn't look like much, but after Gaines's band began holding court on Sunday nights, it became a go-to spot for music lovers of all ages and races. The small storefront with the green exterior and windows covered by burglar bars and a small sign on the eave that reads "Etta's Restaurant 5120 Scott" has been owned by the husband and wife team of Coby and Etta Emery since 1976. Around 1981, Coby and Etta began opening up the back portion of the restaurant to host live bands. Etta's became well known for its delicious fried catfish, much of it caught by Coby himself, mouthwatering burgers, and Sunday-night jams that were off the hook.

Etta Emery, co-owner of Etta's Lounge

WE STARTED OFF as just a soul-food restaurant, and after I retired from nursing and began working there full time, I said (cooking) soul food is too hard for me, so we have to do short orders. That's when we began with the catfish, hamburgers,

French fries, and fried chicken. Later Coby said, "I want some music," because when I met him he used to tap dance. But I didn't want music.

Later on, I started playing on Friday and Saturday nights on Montrose at the River Café for (restaurant owner) Bill Sadler, so I could play at Etta's for free because people that saw me play at River Café wanted to know where they could see me play some more. We started to play more private parties, so the only way they could see me was to come to Etta's. The parking lot was always full on Sunday night; you couldn't even get in for a lot of years. This was the only place where people could see me and let their hair down, so Etta's became one of the well-known restaurants and clubs for a long time.

People from overseas, like Paris and England, would flop in because they had heard about Etta's, and musicians from around town would fin-

Etta Emery, Grady, and Coby Emery in front of Etta's Lounge, 2013. Photo by Rod Evans.

ish their gigs at midnight and flop in for a while and sit in with the band sometimes. Some of the name musicians would drop in when they were in town, too. People like Bobby Bland, Albert Collins, and B. B. King would come through every time they were in town, and Calvin Owens would always stop by. Some of the soul singers that I knew from the road, like Jerry Butler, liked to drop in, too.

Taking over the gig at Etta's was one of the best things I ever did because if I'd stayed on the road I might not be here. I was living a fast life out there. But for a long time, I was working three jobs, which is how I come to have the house where I live now. I was working at the airport sky-capping for American (Airlines), then Continental, then U.S. Air, then United Airlines. I was also working as a bellman at the Holiday Inn and later at the Sheraton. We would finish up at Etta's around one in the morning, and by the time we'd load up and get a hamburger or something it would be around two o'clock. Then I had at least four or five musicians to drop off at their houses, so I would get home around four or four-thirty, and I had to be at work around five. I would sit on the side of the bed, shake my head, and sometimes I'd be a little high, too. I'd go wash my face and get to steppin'. I did that for years, and I'm not sure how I did it, but it paid off for me. I wasn't thinking about working; I was just thinking about doing it. If I thought about the work part, I wouldn't have made it. But I always said at the time, "It ain't nothin' for a stepper."

By me being over the bell staff, I would tell them guys that I'm going to the bathroom and stay in there for twenty or thirty minutes and get some sleep, and I would tell them to cover for me. But I treated them nice, and sometimes I would do the same for them. They saved me a lot by covering for me. I don't know how I did it. I guess it was determination. My mama told me once, "Boy, if you didn't drink, you'd be dead." She said, "I wouldn't go through all that," but I told her, if you want to have a band, this is what you have to do.

Somebody else who also helped me get out there at this time was (guitarist/singer) Jerry Lightfoot, who was real good for the blues musician. He took me around, and I played with him and Pee Wee Stevenson, and we played a lot of little things because he (Lightfoot) paid better than any of them. He talked me up big time, and we played all these old joints that

I had never played before—every little white club in town—and we made pretty good money, too.

> **S**inger/guitarist Jerry Lightfoot, who died in 2006 at age fifty-five, was a fixture on the Houston blues scene in the 1980s and '90s. He and his band, the Essentials, carved out a reputation for putting on electric blues-rock shows at nightclubs all around the area, including the legendary Rockefellers, where they held down the house band gig for a number of years.

I wasn't making a lot of money at Etta's, but I was making money by being there because of the connections. Working at the airport and getting those tips, I had money, so I hired musicians and paid a lot of them out of my pocket. It didn't matter to me. My only interest was building a band, and that's what a bandleader has to go through. I ain't the only one. I'm sure Count Basie and all of them went through their tribulations, too. I must have worked at the airport while playing Etta's on Sunday nights for ten or fifteen years, but I learned so much out there (the airport) by being the transportation manager and meeting a lot of airline pilots and flight attendants and stuff. I learned how to handle my band, and I learned a lot of stuff I use right now.

Etta Emery

SUNDAY NIGHTS WERE REAL GOOD for business. Grady would announce, "Now y'all go get some of them Coby burgers, and Etta's got some of that fish." A lot of the underage college kids would come in, and they couldn't go in the back because we were selling beer back there, so they would ask if they could just stay in here (the main dining area) and listen to the music, and they would fill up all of the seats.

We never did have no problems with the crowds in terms of violence or anything, and they didn't even hire security on Sundays. But, of course, I had a lot of women still, and one night there was a little rumble out in the parking lot, and the police were gonna put one woman in jail. These two women were fighting over me. I guess they wanted some of these good looks! Once the police got there, I went out to the parking lot, and the cop that came knew me because he worked under me as a bellman at the Holiday Inn before he became a policeman, and he let her go.

Coby Emery

THAT WAS THE ONLY VIOLENCE we had all of them years. We had a few women that would come and get a table in front of Grady, and when he'd start playing something like "Something on Your Mind," and he would really get down to it and standing up in the chair and stuff, they would get a little rowdy.

The women would get a little crazy sometimes, but Coby would show up, and it would be all over, and I would just keep on blowing that saxophone. Women would be all over me, fainting and pulling their dresses over their heads and kicking their shoes off. People would get up from their tables and stand there in the aisle and start screaming, "Blow that sax, Grady Gaines!"

The band at this time had Michael Dogan on bass, Floyd Arceneaux on trumpet, Fred Goffney on guitar, Paul David Roberts on trombone and vocals, Lester Hill on baritone sax, Teddy Reynolds on keyboards, Johnny Perry on drums, and Big Robert Smith and Joe Medwick on vocals. That band raised a lot of hell for a long time. I didn't play nowhere unless I had my whole band, and that's my motto. I turned down jobs when they started talking about "Can you cut this or cut that?" That wouldn't be my sound, and I have to have my full band, or you don't get Grady. I have played a handful of solo gigs, but you can count them on one hand.

It didn't take too long (to put the band together) because you had so many good musicians around town; I mean you had a whole lot of cats that could play whatever we were playing. I just picked the ones that I knew I wanted to play with. I wanted my band to be an all-the-way-around band that could play most anything. That way I could get more work.

Big Robert Smith was a big addition to the band early on. He was singing with a group led by Clarence Green, and he told me that Clarence said he couldn't sing. I told him, "Robert, you come with me, and I guarantee we'll make a liar out of 'im," and that's exactly what we did. We had this song called "Strokin'" that Clarence Carter had a hit with first, but everywhere we'd go, Big Robert would tear it up with that song. We really did a heck of a job with that, and people just loved it. We both put that song together, and the arrangement I put on it and the way Robert was doing it gave it a lot of push and fire. Robert, being a big cat like he was, could sing all the blues songs, and he looked the part.

He was clean and sharp and would sing the Junior Parker, Lightnin' Hopkins, and lowdown, dirty blues stuff. He got to be one of the most talked-about vocalists all over the city, and everywhere we went he became a main attraction. He was a house rocker or house shaker, whatever you want to call it. People still ask about him today, and we still miss him. I don't think there'll ever be another Big Robert. Me and him had the same feeling about the blues, and that's why we made such a good team and had such an impact on our fans. Everywhere we played and in so many ways we wanted them (fans) to be a part of us.

At Etta's, Big Robert would sit right by the door during band breaks and would be talking to people as they came in. He became kind of a host on those Sunday nights, and people were coming to see Big Robert almost as much as they were to see me.

Born Robert Lee Smith in Houston's Third Ward, Smith, who weighed in excess of three hundred pounds, died in 2006 at the age of sixty-six. Smith collaborated with many celebrated musicians over the years and fronted his own band—Big Robert and the Ravens—in the '90s. His ballsy, boisterous vocal stylings would be featured prominently on Gaines's three albums released in the late 1980s, early '90s, and '00s.[1]

The Texas Upsetters in the early '90's. From left, Flyod Arceneaux, Big Robert Smith, Earlie Huntsberry Lewis, Michael Dogan, and Grady. Photo from the Grady Gaines Collection.

Joe Medwick did a lot of great stuff over the years, and his name was already out there for all the great songs he wrote for Peacock Records and Bobby Bland, along with so many other artists. He wrote the song "I've Been Out There" that we recorded on my first solo album, *Full Gain*. Even though I'm not a singer, he said he wrote that song about my career and all the things I've done and said I was the only one who could sing it. On most of the shows that Joe did with the band, before he would go into a certain song he would say, "If God made anything better than a woman, he must have kept it for himself." Joe used to tell me, "Grady, I've never seen a saxophone player playing behind three singers, and then when you get out there and do your thing, it's just like the singers were never even there."

Joe Medwick (aka Joe Veasey, Joe Masters, and Joe Melvin) was born Medwick N. Veasey in Houston in 1931. He first came to prominence in the 1950s as a singer and songwriter who worked with many blues and R&B artists of the day and wrote a host of songs for artists recording at Peacock Studios. He wrote or cowrote several popular songs for Bobby "Blue" Bland, including the number-one hit "Further on up the Road," for which he receives half the writing credit. Don Robey, notorious for buying or assuming writing credits and the accompanying publishing royalties from the authors, is listed as cowriter on the track. Medwick died in 1992 at age sixty-one.[2]

Paul David Roberts, who plays trombone and sings, was always important because he could do most anything that I needed in the band, whether it was being an emcee, playing the trombone, or singing. Paul is real talented and is one of the best fill-in cats on that trombone that you will ever find. He can put them little things in the little gaps and make it fit and sound so good. I can't say enough about Paul because he's one of the best trombone players out there and a hell of a talent. He brings a lot of talent to any band. But we had our disagreements, and he didn't always listen to me, so I had to fire him from the band on several occasions. But sometimes husbands and wives have disagreements. It's all about forgive and forget. Forget about it and keep on steppin'.

Paul David Roberts, trombonist/vocalist

PEOPLE WANTED ME FOR MY TROMBONE, but Grady gave me the opportunity to start singing. He's a master at what he does. He knows how to call tunes because he knows how to read the audience, and he knows what he wants. Sometimes I disagree with him, but I learned that he could teach me a whole lot. So, man, I can't talk enough about how he's been a blessing to my experience and has taken me places that were in my dreams. When I first started playing with him, I didn't know nothing about Grady. I just knew that I dug his style, plus he was always dressed impeccably. It was about six months or so after I started playing with him before I knew who he was. I didn't know I was playing with a legend, so that made me more enthusiastic. He was one of the original inventors of rock 'n' roll, but while people know about Little Richard, they don't know about Grady. He's a living legend, and he's still doing what he loves to do. You see, success is not always measured in terms of money. God has blessed me. When I was in the tenth grade, I was looking out the window, and I decided that instead of going the conventional way, working on the job for forty years, I was gonna find a way to enjoy what rich people do through my talent. Grady gave me the opportunity.

Gil Everett was another important part of the band because he could play the blues like nobody else. I mean, he didn't borrow nothing from nobody, and he was the baddest blues guitar player around Houston. When he hit a note, it just went right through you and shook you inside. He was a pretty tall cat, and when he started playing, the house would start trembling.

Before I started the Texas Upsetters and I was playing by myself sometimes, they wanted me to play anywhere they could get me, so I would spot me a rhythm section on one side of town. I would play one gig, leave to go to the next, play that set, then go to the next. I sort of do that now with the whole big band sometimes, too. Our roadies set up three different sound systems, so after the band finishes one gig, we just run to the next, and by the time you finish that last gig, you'll be wore out.

We was still mostly playing at clubs, but we were starting to play a lot of private parties and wedding receptions and stuff at this time. We used to rehearse three times a week, but it all depended on what we needed to catch up on. If we had a lot of songs we needed to catch up on, we rehearsed as many times as we needed to, but most times it was around three times a week. Then we'd get caught up, and I might drop it to two days. We always rehearsed at least one day a week, and Etta's was our rehearsal hall, along with my garage.

I started playing the song "Something on Your Mind" (written by Big Jay McNeely), an instrumental that became my signature song, and everywhere I played it, I demolished the house. One night around 1987 or '88, we were playing it at Rockefeller's (in Houston), and a guy named Bob Bell, who was the manager for (blues band) Roomful of Blues, saw me and really liked the band. He told me after the show that he knew these people in New Orleans who ran a record company called Black Top Records. He said "I'm gonna tell 'em about you and get them to come here and see you the next time you play here."

He got in touch with them, and these two brothers, Nauman and Hammond Scott, both came in to town and caught us at Rockefeller's. We played "Something on Your Mind" and tore up the house, and when I came off stage, they said, "We're gonna record you." It was Grady Gaines and the Upsetters at this time, but Hammond wanted to get the rest of Texas in front of it, so that's when it became Grady Gaines and the Texas Upsetters.

Hammond and Nauman Scott, two music-loving brothers from Alexandria, Louisiana, founded New Orleans's Black Top Records around 1980. A lawyer, Hammond Scott was working as an assistant district attorney under Orleans Parish District Attorney Harry Connick Sr., the father of Grammy Award–winning singer and actor Harry Connick Jr., when he and his brother decided to launch Black Top Records. The company started out as primarily a blues label, but the Scott brothers would expand its artist lineup to include New Orleans R&B and American roots music acts. Black Top's first release was the 1981 album *Talk to You by Hand* by Anson Funderburgh and the Rockets.

Lovers of blues and R&B music, Hammond and Nauman especially delighted in finding new talent or rediscovering veteran acts who had slid out of the limelight. It was primarily Hammond, who had been involved in music off and on for years, who worked directly with the artists, while Nauman, a federal judge in the US District Court for the Western District of Louisiana, handled the business side of the company. In the early 1970s Hammond even quit law school at Tulane University to become the personal manager, road manager, and booking agent for legendary blues artist Clarence "Gatemouth" Brown. After working with the mercurial Brown from 1974 to 1978, Hammond returned to law school at Tulane, got his degree, and then went to work in the DA's office. Nauman died in 2002.

Hammond says Black Top Records was founded as a means to

help him keep a foot in the door of the music industry. Hammond, who hosted a blues radio program on WWOZ radio in New Orleans prior to starting the label, says his desire to properly record veteran blues artists to allow their true talent to shine was the impetus for starting the label. Black Top issued about two records per year in its early years, but by the early 1990s, production had increased to six to eight titles per year, with distribution first handled by Rounder Records and later by Passport Music and Alligator Records. The lineup of Black Top artists included Snooks Eaglin, Earl King, Roomful of Blues, Guitar Shorty, Anson Funderburgh and the Rockets, Ronnie Earl, Solomon Burke, the Neville Brothers, and Maria Muldaur.

Black Top Records ceased operation in 1999 after releasing more than one hundred albums when the brothers sold its catalog to Universal Entertainment. Some of Black Top's releases were reissued by labels such as Hep Cat, Verese Sarabande, Fuel 2000, and Shout! Factory. The Japanese label P-Vine in 2006 acquired the rights to the catalog and has released a few reissues since then. Hammond, now sixty-three, works as a financial planner with Ameriprise Financial in Metairie, Louisiana.

Hammond Scott, co-owner of Black Top Records, 1980–1999

I SAW GRADY way before I knew who he was. It must have been sometime in the early 1970s, when T-Bone Walker made a trip back to Houston after not playing there for twenty or thirty years and had a one-week run at a club there. Grady was there and got up and played. I thought he was very handsome, exotic looking. He looked sort of Arabian or something because he was wearing a sultanlike outfit, but I didn't know who he was at the time. (Around 1986–1987) Greg Piccolo with Roomful of Blues called and told me about the show Grady had and that it was an old-school R&B show with horns and multiple singers and a real stage show and that we should come see Grady and his band the next time they played at Rockefellers.

Me and Nauman came to Houston for the show, and Grady was all over the stage and had this powerhouse blast of a sound. Back then he was a house rocker. In fact, I actually heard Gatemouth talk about Grady, and he described him as a house rocker with a big tenor sound. I'd say about thirty days after meeting Grady we decided to do the album.

A great thing that happened around 1986 was I met Clemet Nell Pharms when I was playing at Etta's. We were loading up the van after the gig, and she came walking through the place where you turn your ticket in to go back where we played. I ran into Nell, we got to talking, and that was the beginning. We been hooked up ever since. So you see, Etta's Lounge was a great place in more ways than one for me. Out of all the women I had met in my life, God put in store for me Miss Clemet Nell Pharms.

Nell Pharms, Grady's wife

GRADY GAVE ME HIS NUMBER, and I never called him. I kept his number for about six months and never called him, so he called me. I had gone to the store, but a friend staying at my house told me I'd gotten a call. I had a private number and only remember giving it to one guy, so I called Grady and asked him "Did you call?" He tried to lie his way out of it, but he finally confessed. He had tried to get me to come home with him that first night, but I said "uh uh." He had to play a gig that Sunday in Corpus Christi, and he wanted me to go with him. I said OK and that was it. I had a brother that used to hang out at Etta's a lot, and I had been there a few times but had never seen Grady play. It was "Something on Your Mind" that kept me coming back there. I told my sister there's this guy playing this song, and it don't sound real when he's doing it. It sounds fantastic! The more I heard it, the more I wanted to keep coming back to hear it. When he played that song, all them girls used to gather around Grady in a circle, and that used to make me so angry that I couldn't stand it. I'd ease my way between 'em and do my

little snake dance, and them girls would move all the way back. I
remember he was playing at this one club, and he got on the floor
on his back and played the saxophone. Well, this girl tried to sit
on his face. Grady shot up and said, "You ain't sittin' on my face!"
Sometimes I would have to leave out the room, but I guess I've
run 'em all off now.

We was busy nonstop, and my phone never stopped ringing. One night
(around 1988) we were at the Mucky Duck (venerable Houston nightclub, McGonigel's Mucky Duck), I think, and it was raining like cats and
dogs. Bill Sadler (owner of the River Café) was there, and so was Nell.
He said, I know this booking agent, Susan Criner of Gulf Coast Artists
(now Gulf Coast Entertainment). He told Susan about me, so she and
her husband came around to see us one evening, and then we had dinner,
where we talked about different things, and she asked me all kinds of
questions, and I answered them. We were just sort of picking each other's
mind about what we knew about the business. She said she wanted to
start booking me, and I said, "You're just what I need, and I've been hearing a lot of good talk about you." From that day on I've been with Susan.

At the time, every (booking) agency in town was trying to get me, but
after I got with Susan, I told people, I'll play those jobs, but you got to go
through Susan, and that's the only way I'll play 'em. I'm not going to get
out there and get mixed up with two or three jobs booked here and two
or three jobs booked there. I said it's got to be one person handling me,
and that will be Susan Criner. After that, all the agencies started going
through her, and they all get their percentage, whatever it is. I didn't care
so long as I didn't get nothing mixed up. All I wanted to do was arrive
(at a gig) with no problems. She's the best booking agent in town by a
long shot. They used to call James Brown the hardest-working man in
show business, but I call her the hardest-working woman in the booking
business.

Susan Criner, booking agent, president of Gulf Coast Entertainment

I MET GRADY when he played at Rockefellers with Roomful of Blues. I was just blown away! At that time I had an ongoing booking agency called the Party Company. I hadn't changed the name to Gulf Coast Entertainment yet. Grady was definitely a project for me. I saw a lot of potential in him and thought he was the perfect crossover band for the private-party market, which I was just developing. That included debutante parties, weddings, and charity galas, and I knew they would love him, and they have. He's been working really hard at those corporate and social events but not to the exclusion of some great clubs and festivals, like the Great Taste of Houston, the Houston International Festival, and Galveston's Mardi Gras. I knew the material he was playing—all of that great '50s', '60s', and '70s' music—was what the private-party segment was looking for. I asked if I could help with his calendar. I've never been comfortable with the term "manager" because I feel like a manager for an artist is a full-time job, and I have a full-time job. I wanted to coordinate his calendar and make sure his contracts are in order. I do all of his payments, so all of the money comes through us, so it's clean and correct, and the accounting is correct. I also signed him up for ASCAP so he would have the means to get some royalties, and I think he's gotten a couple of checks, which is more than he ever got before.

After we started playing at the River Café, it turned out to be real popular to where you couldn't hardly get in the door on most nights. We wasn't making much money there, but it helped me make connections with people to start playing some real big weddings and private parties.

Bill Sadler, owner of River Café, 1984–1989

I HAD BUILT A MUSIC ROOM that seated about forty to sixty people maximum at the River Café and was looking for music to put into it. I was gonna put jazz in there, but somebody told me about these guys that were playing at Etta's that I just had to see. I went to Etta's and heard them (the Texas Upsetters), and they blew me away. I'd never seen anything like it in my life, and everybody in the room went crazy. Grady was up on chairs swayin' back and forth while he played, and I said, "This is what I want!" I knew within five minutes of seeing them that this was better than anything I could hope for. That first night they played at my place they had seven or eight musicians take the stage, and nobody knew what to expect, but they couldn't help but go crazy. They put on a great show, and they were great guys, so they were wildly popular from the start. You could get a chair pretty easy that first night, but after that it got pretty tough. I'll never forget that first night they played there, and these guys (the Upsetters) were used to being at some pretty tough venues in the day over in the Fifth Ward and Third Ward, but now they're in the Montrose, where we're all peace, love, and happiness. Well, they started opening their (instrument) cases, and Big Robert had the biggest pistol I'd ever seen. Somebody had a razor. Somebody had a knife. I told them, "Guys, I don't think you're gonna need these here."

The crowd started out being mostly what I'd guess you'd call a hippie crowd, but my dinner clientele was more upscale, and these wealthy people started coming to Grady's shows and just took it over. All these trust-fund babies were going crazy in there. I don't think white Houston had ever seen anything like this, and it just blew them away to be in the room with that level of energy and talent. They didn't realize this was available in Houston because these wealthy River Oaks white people had been insulated from that. We had all kinds of people coming in, like (actress) Cloris Leachman, who was in town for a while and came in to listen almost every night they played. (Actor) Dennis Hopper (who died in 2010) came in and listened one night. I left there over twenty-five years ago, and hardly a week goes by that somebody doesn't come up to me and say, "Remember when Grady Gaines and the Texas Upsetters were playing there?"

There was another club we played on Montrose after we left the River Café called the Sierra Grill. We went in there, and there was nothing going on, and we played every Wednesday and sometimes on Saturday if we didn't have a wedding or something, but most of the time we had a wedding every Saturday. We started playing in there, and it started picking up and started getting so crowded where you couldn't get in there. We played from ten until two, and it'd be jam-packed. We had lines three deep from the club door all the way back to where the Goodyear (auto repair shop) was; that's almost half a block. This went on for years, and all we were getting was $300 a night. People thought I was making all kinds of money.

But I looked at things like this: It was a place where my booking agent could send wedding couples that wanted to hear the band before they hired them, so I looked at it in the long run and said I might not get it here with the $300, but I get it in another way. And believe me, I got it in another way.

But playing them private parties is different from playing the clubs. In the clubs, you can just throw down and pretty much play what you want to play, but when you're playing a private party, you have a guide of songs to go by. You might have to play three or four different kinds of music depending on what they want. We might start off a wedding reception playing sweet music like Sinatra or Duke Ellington's "Satin Doll" or Billie Holiday or Nat King Cole while they're eating. After they finish eating, they want to dance, so we pick up the tempo. But it also depends on the ages of the people there. If there's a lot of old people, maybe people around my age, we might play some music from the '50s, for example. Then as the night goes on, you start to pick and choose and take some requests, and by the end of the night, you're playing some music for the younger people because they'll be the last to leave. But not every band can do what we do because my repertoire goes from the '30s all the way up to today, and you've got to be a good crowd reader.

Playing the private parties pays way more than the clubs. In those early days, if we made $35, $40, or $50 (per band member) playing a club, that was a good gig. When we first started playing weddings and stuff, $1,500 (total) was good, but now, shit, we make pretty close to $4,000 and up. But it's (private parties) harder work—more tedious work. You've got to do everything right on time, and it ain't like where you just go there and play. It's a lot like a real job. But our set list came off the top of my head. I'd always start with a theme song and maybe three or four tunes in a row, and I'd tell them (the band) what tunes I was gonna do. We'd be there (at the venue) setting up, and I'd look at the crowd and kind of see what I needed to do. All through the night I'd call three or four songs at a time, and I'd have in the back of my mind what was coming up next as time passed, and I'd call whichever one I needed, and I'd do that all night long. Still do.

Paul David Roberts

GRADY WOULD ALWAYS DRESS APPROPRIATELY because a band has to look good. A lot of bands would get off of work and keep on their brogans and come to the gig, but Grady was always first class. One time we had a set of five tuxedos, and he would have Caldwell Tailors make special shirts for us. He always insisted that his band be dressed. When I first started playing with Grady, I wasn't used to playing in tuxedos, and we were playing in Galveston. Me and a drummer, a cat named Julius, who was with us at the time, were standing outside the door, and this white lady drove up and said, "You boys come and get this food out of my trunk." Me and Julius looked at each other and shuffled on down, and she gave us a $10 tip. She thought we were the doormen because she wasn't used to seeing black band members dressed like that.

Me and Big Robert used to ride day in and day out all over town to all the places where they sell tuxedos. After so long, they'd put them out into the Goodwill stores, so we would ride to every Goodwill store we could and other places until we found all the sizes that we needed. Every time we'd find one, we'd get it right then. We did that for a long time. It was costing me time and money, but I didn't mind doing it. Plus, if I got a band that cooperates with me like those guys did . . . we were like a family and that makes a big difference. The band I have now, it seems like there's at least three families in it. That's what I have to deal with now, but I guarantee you I handle it very well.

CHAPTER 11

In the Studio

It turned out that the Scott brothers were serious about recording me. I hadn't really thought much about making my own album, but I had been doing things like that for a long time, like putting a band or a show together.

It took about a week at (Houston's) Sugar Hill Recording Studio (in 1987) to record the *Full Gain* album (Black Top, 1988). I had some stuff in my head that I needed to get out, so once you get to thinking like that, it just starts flowing. You do one thing, then something else comes to light. Doing the album was one of the best feelings I ever had. I always thought about the other person (artist) and never did think about me doing a recording. I felt good about what we were doing because I had all these cats that I thought so much about and grew up together with on there.

The album included cover tunes and originals. When it came to choosing the cover tunes, it just had to be something I liked and felt good about playing; it didn't have to be a particular artist; if I felt like we could do something with it, then we'd take a shot at it.

When I listened to *Full Gain*, it came out just the way I wanted it to because I had just the right musicians on there. Clarence (Holliman) was one of the best guitar players around and played on a lot of the Peacock Records stuff. I had Roy, and I knew if I had all three of us, we were going to have a good CD, plus in the horn section, I had Floyd (Arceneaux), who was a terrific trumpet player, arranger, and writer, and Conrad Johnson played alto sax in the reed section. Ron Levy played organ. We had Lloyd Lambert on bass, and we had two drummers—Walter Joseph and David Lee—and Teddy Reynolds on keyboards. I had Kaz Kazanoff on baritone sax and Paul David Roberts on trombone. Big Robert Smith and Joe Medwick were the main vocalists.

Released in 1988, *Full Gain* was produced by Hammond Scott, with assistance from Roy Gaines. A look at the track list reveals that ten of the twelve songs were originals written by people who appeared on the album. Joe Medwick wrote or cowrote four songs ["I've Been Out There," "If I Don't Get Involved (I Can't Get Hurt)," "If I Loved You a Little Less," and "Your Girlfriend."] Roy Gaines provided three songs (the CD opener, "Mr. Blues in the Sky," "Stealing Love," and "Gangster of the Blues." Grady Gaines gets songwriting credit on the title track, and Teddy Reynolds wrote "Shaggy Dog" and "Miss Lucy Brown." Of course, the album includes "Something on Your Mind," which had become Grady's signature song. According to Hammond Scott, *Full Gain* was produced for $25,000 to $30,000 and sold about ten thousand copies.

Hammond Scott, co-owner of Black Top Records and producer on Full Gain.

GRADY HAD THE IDEA to bring his brother in, and when he said he wanted Clarence Holliman on the record, I was surprised. I had heard of Clarence from his Duke-Peacock Records days, so he was one of those names I knew, and Grady knew where he could put a hand on him. The first time I came to Houston to meet with Grady before the sessions, he took me to meet Clarence, and a funny thing happened. Clarence was living in an apartment complex with his wife, (singer) Carol Fran. She actually did an audition for me on the spot. She was cooking a hamburger for me and singing a cappella, and I recorded it with a little portable cassette deck I used to carry with me. I wish I could find that tape because it was terrific. She ultimately became a Black Top artist.

The sessions went well, but there were some issues. Grady had Johnny Perry, who was a deaf drummer, so that was a hindrance right there. He could do a good job in live appearances because he could see all the signals he needed to see, but the studio was a little tougher.

The studio was a little smaller than I would have liked to use because with a little larger room things could breathe a little bit more. We had a lot of (sound) leakage on purpose because we were trying to have that live sound, but we had more leakage than we wanted because of how small the room was and how little isolation they had. We brought in upright bass player Lloyd Lambert from New Orleans, a great player who had played with Guitar Slim. But we had so much sound bleeding through the upright that I never got the bottom that I wanted to have. We had Grady's bass player (Michael Dogan), who was good on some things and on certain things he learned from Lloyd.

A big problem was Grady wanted to use another drummer, but that drummer got arrested during the session for nonsupport, and that created a real problem. Apparently he had talked too much and said where he was going to be when he was at the studio, so the cops knew where to arrest him. He hadn't even warmed up before he was arrested. Walter Joseph came in on drums, but it didn't look like he would work for the whole record, so we started calling people in New Orleans. Of course, this is a terrible position to be in in the middle of a session, so we also started trying to think of people in Houston we could use. We started relying on Roy for some of that, but Roy would say about a guy, "Nah, he's more of a jazz drummer. If you say shuffle to him, he'll play a cute shuffle." We eventually had to fly David Lee in from New Orleans, who was a jazz drummer with a light touch, but he had more of what we were looking for.

This was the first time that me and Roy had really recorded together even though we did some things at Peacock, but this was the first *real* session. Because Roy went out on the road when he was so young, we never had much chance to record together. Roy was based in New York for a long time, but now he's in Los Angeles, but even though we always seemed to be on opposite sides of the country, we've always kept in close contact.

Roy Gaines

FOR A LONG TIME, Grady was busy and I was busy, but when we saw each other, we would have one heck of a good time. Recording Grady's album was one of those good times, and it was what I'd been dreaming could have happened. I always thought we could create another "Texas sound." Maybe call it the "longhorn sound" or something. I had this idea for a record company called QBR Productions that would do records that were a musical soup. We would have Grady playing those long tones on the sax—those honkin'-type solos. I believe if it had been financed, we could have had the same kind of success that Robey had with Peacock. We would have been doing music that was a split between Motown, Houston blues, Little Richard, Sam Cooke, and Little Willie John—all the stuff that Grady brought to the table, plus all the things I brought from Chuck Willis, Brook Benton, Ray Charles, and Billie Holiday.

The song "I've Been Out There" was the first song recorded during the *Full Gain* sessions. Written by Grady's longtime friend Joe Medwick and sung by Grady, it chronicles Grady's career and life on the road and features Gaines rattling off the names of notable artists he's performed with such as B. B. King, James Brown, and Etta James in a talking-singing style that somehow seems appropriate for the song.

Hammond Scott

GRADY HAD BROUGHT IN other horn players but didn't have the rhythm section nailed down when we started recording, so I thought it was overkill having the horn players sitting around to record the horn section live before the rhythm section. The only place on the record where all the horn players played was "I've Been Out There," so we decided to record it first. But I thought we were going to have a train wreck at first.

Roy did the arrangement on the song and played one of my favorite guitar solos on the album. It's just a fabulous solo—a very modern solo. Grady was excited to sing the song, but we had to come to terms with the fact that he is not a singer, so he sort of talked through it. He was committed to doing it, and he knows he's not a singer, but the song didn't require him to be Sam Cooke. We had the upright and electric bass on the track, and you can feel the upright, but you can't really hear it. For a funkier song like that, the bass line is lighter than we wanted because of the leakage, so we had to mix the two bass parts together, but I would've liked a heavier bottom on it.

Teddy Reynolds was another strong suit that Grady had. It wasn't so much about him trying to be a soloist—because he didn't solo very often—but he had good song ideas and was a great asset in the band. Floyd Arceneaux was a great musician, too, and very dependable in the studio.

One of my favorite songs on the album is "If I Don't Get Involved (I Can't Get Hurt)," which was written and sung by Joe Medwick. I thought it was a pretty heavy arrangement. It had a perfect feel to it, but Joe had a couple of mistakes that we had to call him on, so he went back and resang it. If you listen closely, you can hear a little leakage in a couple of spots, and it almost sounds like somebody is saying something in the background.

The song came together really fast with the two guitars on there, and I love the way they work together, especially in the turnarounds. That's what's missing in the version Bobby "Blue" Bland covered (*Midnight Run*, Malaco, 1988). The guitar turnarounds are missing, and, to me, that takes a lot of the punch out of it. Now, you had Bobby Bland singing, and that's great, but I like our version better.

Hammond Scott and Grady at release party for the *Full Gain* album, Houston, 1988. Photo from the Grady Gaines Collection.

We were playing almost every night at this point, sometimes eight or nine times a week with double gigs. We might play three times on a Saturday, maybe three weddings in one day. I was still picking up most of the musicians before gigs, so I'd have to leave early in the morning to get to these different hotels, country clubs, and ballrooms so the roadies could set up the sound system. But we didn't want to let no job go, and they wanted the band bad enough that they would book us no matter how they could get us, and I didn't want to let none of our clients down.

Hammond (Scott) wanted me to travel all the time (to support the album), but I said, "What am I gonna do when I can't travel no more?" He was right in a sense, but I had to think about me at a later age. The more you travel if you have a record out, the more it helps to sell the record. But blues wasn't making as much money as I was playing these private parties and different stuff, plus I wouldn't have to go nowhere. I told him I'll record for you as long as you have a record company, and I'll make some dates, but it all has to correspond with this office (Gulf Coast

Entertainment). That's the deal I made. Most of the dates we did were around Houston, Dallas–Fort Worth, and Louisiana, so we did travel, but I could usually be home every night or the next day.

We did do a tour of California right after *Full Gain* came out, and the first city we hit was Los Angeles, and at first we couldn't find a hotel, but we finally found one out there in San Pedro. We checked in and were there overnight, and (when) we came back to the van to leave for San Diego for a show with (legendary blues producer, arranger, and bassist) Willie Dixon and some other people, we got in and saw that the whole dashboard had been taken out! They'd robbed us and took everything. We rented another van and some equipment, went on down the road, and did the show.

I always like to pay the musicians in advance. Most people don't, but I didn't like to deal with all that after the show. Well, after I'd paid the band off in San Pedro, we got down to San Diego, and our bass player at the time got so high he couldn't even stand up—couldn't do nothing. I had to figure out how to get him sober, so we took some ice cubes and put 'em on his nuts for ten or fifteen minutes! Our trumpet player, Lamar Wright from New York, told me about the ice cubes thing. He finally got to where he could play the show, but that was the only way we could play because, without a bass player, you could make the job, but you'd have a much harder time doing it.

Robert "Little Robert" Lewis, Texas Upsetters driver and road manager and husband of Upsetters singer Earlie Huntsberry Lewis

LOTS OF TIMES band members would get drunk, and that was against Grady's rules. Period. If you had a problem with Grady, he'd take care of it himself, and he didn't mind getting down with you. I was on an elevator one time, and Big Robert Smith was talking a lot of smack, and Grady handled it. He was the kindest man, and you wouldn't think he'd scrap with you, but if you crossed him . . . business is business, you know? Michael Dogan used to always talk a lot, and we'd be driving, and Grady would say, "Little Robert, pull this van over," and Mike Dogan would get out, and the van would take off. We'd be in the middle of the highway, and he'd run so Grady couldn't get hold of him. It wasn't just Mike, though. If he had a problem, he'd tell me to "pull the van over. I got a problem in here," and all that stuff would stop.

Hammond Scott

GRADY NEVER WAS ABLE to be on the road all the time, and I'm kinda glad he didn't because he'd probably be dead now because it's so grueling. But we made a great tour of California, where we were out there for about six weeks and went up and down the coast playing some great clubs. One story I remember from that tour was we were driving on the Pacific Coast Highway in some pretty high (elevation) areas, and Big Robert Smith didn't like heights. When we were in areas where there were woods on the side of the road, he was OK, but he didn't like being able to see how high we were.

Anyway, we had pulled over to the side of the road, and Big Robert was in the front seat and had the window down. I walked over there and saw him having a snack. He had a big industrial-size jar of mayonnaise and was eating it off a big spoon. I said, "Man, that makes me sick! How can you do that to yourself?" It was hot, and I thought, this stuff is gonna get hot, and he's gonna get sick, but he had a damp towel around his neck and was happy.

A few miles down the road, though, we got into some roads where you looked over cliffs, and we pulled over again, but this time it was different. He wasn't eating that mayonnaise, and he had the towel over his head and face. Being up that high scared the hell out of him.

On that same trip, we went down to where the Hearst Castle is located (in San Simeon, California), and me and my brother wanted to pull over and tour the castle. Some of the guys just wanted to hurry up and get some wine at the next stop; that's all they were concerned about. Well, Grady put it up for a vote to see who wanted to see the castle and who wanted to keep going.

Joe Medwick said, "I seen all the castles I wanna see in them Vincent Price movies," and that took care of that. We didn't get to see the castle.

Things was going real good for the band at this time with the record out and everything, but in April of 1989 my mother had a stroke and died (at age seventy-nine). It was one of the worst times of my life. She was so important in all of our lives for so long, so it was just a sad occasion for everybody in our family, but like when Daddy died those years before, the family came together and dealt with everything and buried her in Houston.

Not too long after my mother passed, our next album, *Blues-a-Rama* (Black Top, 1990), was recorded at Tipitina's in New Orleans, and I put the album together like if I would be doing a show. I would open with my theme song, then play the opening number, "Let Your Thing Hang Down," before bringing each singer (Medwick, Smith, and Roberts) on, and let them do two to three songs. We just did what we had been doing for years at gigs, and the people loved it everywhere we played. The Scott brothers watched us play live quite a few times and said they wanted to cut a live CD with us, and it turned out to be one of my best CDs. We had it all together because it was the way we did it on stage, but a lot of stuff just happened spontaneously, and we kind of cleaned it up in the studio.

Recorded in 1989, *Blues-a-Rama: Live, Down & Dirty* was produced by Hammond and Nauman Scott with postproduction work done at Houston's Sugar Hill Studios. The sprawling disc features eighteen tracks that are grouped revue-style into six segments, with singers Paul David Roberts, Joe Medwick, and Big Robert Smith serving as the featured singers of their own segments, along with instrumentals grouped under the Upsetters' banner.

Hammond Scott

I LOVED GRADY'S LIVE SHOW because it had an old style to it with all the (song) chaser things, and there was never a dead moment. As soon as somebody finished, the band would go into this theme music. It was recorded in one night at Tipitina's. Grady had the show well paced and knew what he wanted the set to be. We chopped some stuff out, but it was pretty much like a live gig. It probably sold the least of Grady's albums, but we felt like we captured the live show well. Joe Medwick was still around, and Paul David Roberts was always great as a singer and musician, and Big Robert acquitted himself well.

For *Horn of Plenty* (Black Top, 1992), we recorded in New Orleans. I had a lot of different musicians, but some of the same people from *Full Gain* were on there, too. I had arranger "Kaz" Kazanoff again, who brought a different flavor, and both of our ideas came together well. The cat I was really in love with on the record was organ player Sammy Berfect.

Horn of Plenty was recorded in 1992 at Ultrasonic Studios in New Orleans, and the Scott brothers again served as producers. In addition to the regular band, the album included guest appearances by celebrated New Orleans bassist George Porter Jr. of legendary funk/R&B band the Meters, as well as acclaimed blues guitarist Anson Funderburgh. The album was dedicated to the memory of Joe Medwick and Floyd Arceneaux, both of whom died during the two years separating the release of *Blues-a-Rama* and *Horn of Plenty.*

Hammond Scott

ON *Horn of Plenty* Grady wanted to somehow or another try to use all of his horn players on it, but we had a hard time in the studio, and it was not coming together because we were trying to create new tunes. So I had everybody stand down except the frontline players and brought in George Porter on bass and Herman Ernest on drums, who was Dr. John's drummer. We also brought in Sammy Berfect on organ and piano. He's no longer living, but he led more black gospel choirs in New Orleans than anybody. As soon as we got everybody in place, the first song we recorded, "Baby, Work Out," the groove was there, and we recorded it in one take. It was a fun record to make and went pretty quickly.

In 1992, after *Horn of Plenty* came out, we did a thirty-one-day tour of Europe with Fats Domino, and we got paid well, but so many groups had started going over there, and they (promoters) would get anybody that could play a little blues or whatever and bring them over. That would be their first time doing that, so they could get 'em for a real cheap price, and that started interfering with me getting the type of money I wanted to get paid. It's too much traveling, too. It's not as easy as people think it is. Once you get over there, moving from date to date, they have it as comfortable as possible, but I still wasn't as excited about it as most people would be.

It was a nice feeling touring with my own album. We played all of the songs on the album and tore it up over there. We opened for Fats and finished the set with "Something on Your Mind," and at one gig they called the band back to the stage at least seven times, and they were still trying to get me to play more, but you get tired after playing so long, and that was when I was in good shape, and the arthritis hadn't caught up with me. They wanted more, more, more and were just hollerin', so we did a fast chaser and got off of there. My band and Fats' band were always good friends, and we had a heck of a time on the tour riding around Europe in those big Mercedes buses.

It was a nice feeling to play gigs after the album came out, but I had toured all my life, so it wasn't new to me other than it was my own album. But while being in Europe excited most people in the band, it didn't excite me as much. I mean, I liked being over there for thirty-one days with Fats, but when I got back to IAH (Houston's Bush Intercontinental

Airport), I kissed the ground. Not that I hated it (touring in Europe)—because I loved what we did and how they (European audiences) accepted us—it's just me flying over all that water . . .

Joe "Guitar" Hughes made the European tour with Fats with us and had a spot on the show and had a lot to do with the "Live at Tipitina's" *(Blues-a-Rama)* album. When we played behind Sam Cooke, I called Joe and got him on the road with us. He stayed out there a long time when we was backing Sam.

After that tour, me and Paul saw Fats and did a session. We were down at Cosmo's Studio in New Orleans, and Fats Domino came in there. He was setting up to do his Christmas (CD) session, and he saw us and said, "Oooh, them people overseas sure do love y'all. They're just crazy about y'all." He gave me a $20 bill and autographed it, and I gave it to my girlfriend, and she framed it.

Paul David Roberts

> HE (FATS DOMINO) had a separate apartment on his house because he loved to cook, and his wife wouldn't allow him to cook in the main house. He cooked some gumbo. If you saw the (TV) special on (Hurricane) Katrina (a documentary titled "Fats Domino: Walking Back to New Orleans"), he walked through his house, and everything was destroyed. He hasn't been heard from since, really. He used to keep his awards and stuff in that separate apartment, but he practically collapsed in the man's arms (on TV) because his house was destroyed.

Fats Domino has, in fact, been seen since Katrina damaged his home. In 2007 he headlined a benefit concert at Tipitina's to raise money to help those left homeless by the hurricane. The documentary "Fats Domino: Walking Back to New Orleans" records the concert, during which Domino performed a short set of his biggest hits. Domino, who turned eighty-five in 2013, has not performed publicly since but still makes a few appearances around his hometown of New Orleans.[1]

Earlie Huntsberry Lewis, Texas Upsetters vocalist

WE TOURED FIVE COUNTRIES in Europe, and I was the only female, but the band treated me with nothing but the grandest respect. I remember we were in some little town in France, and everybody in the band was sick, like they all came down with the flu. So I went next door to a store and bought some stuff to make some soup for everybody. We had just gotten to France, but we didn't miss a single gig. We were doing a series of one-nighters, and the only place we stayed two weeks was in Paris, at the Le Méridien Hotel. We played the Lionel Hampton Room. As a little girl, I always wanted to stand on the Eiffel Tower, and I got to do that, so I always told Grady he made a little girl's dreams come true. The crowds were just beautiful and appreciated us so much that I wished I could have imported them here. We signed autographs, and we never did that here. The crowds were huge, too. If we played a stadium, it would be full, and if it was a theater, it was full. The Hampton Room stayed packed for all six nights we played there. Grady came up with the idea that since it was April, we should make our theme "April in Paris," and it was beautiful the way we opened the show with the song "April in Paris."

On the tour of Europe, we were over there with a bunch of other artists, including Jimmy "T-99" Nelson, Joe Louis Walker, and about six or seven other bands. When we got through with the tour, they had a big party for us, and they had a table in this dining room that ran from one end of the room to the other. They had whole hogs, chicken, turkey, everything. It was in this castle, and it was just like you see in those movies where the king be at his table, and there was all kinds of food and drink—anything you could think of—and I was the star of the show. It was crazy.

We had a real good time overseas, but I tell you what, ain't nothing like the United States for me. But I had a good time there. After a gig, I would usually go to my room and stay there, but Paul and Big Robert just be getting started. They'd go back out and hit the streets for the clubs and the fun. They didn't want to miss anything.

Earlie Huntsberry Lewis

WHILE WE WERE PLAYING PARIS, a doctor invited the band to dinner, and you know their customs are different than ours. I was trying to tell the guys that, at the end of each meal, they're going to offer bread, wine, and cheese, and it's an insult if you don't eat and drink some. It wasn't that I'd ever been there before; I just read a lot. Well, another one of their customs is when they cook chicken, they don't cut the head off and just cook the whole chicken. Now, Big Robert was afraid of chickens; I mean it was serious for him, so when the waiter brought the chicken on the platter and set it down near where Big Robert was sitting, he seriously freaked out and wanted to run from the table. We had to explain to them that he was afraid of chickens, and they moved the platter to the other end of the table. Big Robert loved to eat chicken, but he wouldn't eat any of *that* chicken. It was hilarious! Here was Big Robert, a big, three-hundred-pound masculine guy who was not a wimp, but he wasn't eating none of that chicken. As you can imagine, the rest of the guys kidded him about that forever.

There was another time when we were on a plane that was landing in Nice (France). Because it's right on the water, when the plane made a bank to the right, it went right over the ocean, and it looked like the tip of the wing was gonna hit the water. Big Robert and Michael Dogan started screaming about the plane going down, and Dogan was telling Robert, "If you sit down maybe the plane won't lean so far that way." They went back and forth with each other, and the rest of us were just laughing our heads off.

Grady was pretty quiet on the road and didn't do a whole lot of sightseeing. I called him "boss man" because that's always been his demeanor, and he carried himself in a professional man- ner everywhere we went. He didn't do a lot of running around because that type of travel didn't excite him like it did us. We were like kids in the candy store. Every now and then he'd ask me if I was going to a store, and he'd give me some money to buy some souvenirs for him to take back home, but he didn't lolly-gag or shoot the breeze much because he was meeting with the promoters and stuff like that to take care of business. He was making sure when we left one hotel to go to another that everything was ready, and he made sure I always had a dressing room.

Paul David Roberts

MY FAVORITE CITY was Amsterdam because I never dreamed I could walk off in a restaurant, and they hand you a menu of the wine they were selling and a menu of the different marijuana they were selling. Plus, you didn't see cops wearing guns or people being arrested. It was quite an experience.

We played a lot of dates in Texas, Louisiana, and Oklahoma after the European tour. Then we got booked to play the Chicago Blues Festival. We did so well there that they booked us two years in a row, and it was unusual to have an artist back for a second year.

We picked up right where we left off, but we did have a couple of incidents along the way. Like I said, I had to fire Paul on several occasions, and I'd let him come back because he's a hell of a talent, but we bumped heads, and he would just do some crazy stuff sometimes. One of those things was when we'd play weddings and women would take their shoes off, Paul would take some of those shoes. He just had the devil in him, I guess, and he would sell 'em. I would have to go through all kinds of stuff with the (booking agent) office to try and locate the shoes and explain what happened. But we would always straighten it out.

Greg Gormanous has known Grady on a professional and personal level for more than twenty-nine years. A licensed psychologist living in Alexandria, Louisiana, Gormanous has conducted what he calls "psychohistory" studies on numerous blues and R&B performers, including B. B. King and Steve Cropper, in addition to Grady. He says an artist's psychohistory looks at "impactful events that took place when they were young in life and how that impacted who they became in terms of their identity." He formerly taught psychology at Louisiana State University at Alexandria and now works as a consultant in the field of entertainment psychology.

Greg Gormanous, Grady's longtime friend

I MET GRADY through the Scott brothers, who are from Alexandria, around 1993. I was trying to find talent to help revise the Cenla (Central Louisiana) Celebration music festival in Alexandria and told Nauman (Scott) I needed some top talent. I had just stumbled across Grady's *Blues-a-Rama* CD and just fell in love with it, and Nauman suggested I book him for the festival, which I did, and Grady was just so easy to work with. I vividly remember that David Duke, the racist former Klansman, was running for governor of Louisiana against Edwin Edwards at the time. Back then they allowed political groups to organize at festivals, and I'll never forget that Grady Gaines and the Texas Upsetters had David Duke supporters dancing with blacks under a tent. The mayor asked me, "How does he do that?" and I said, "It's the power of music. It's the universal language." That was a magical moment because that was a very divisive race in Louisiana.

That was the first time I'd seen Grady perform, and he and the band were dynamite. Grady's tone is like a meat grinder that thumps! We had twenty-eight to thirty acts booked for the festival, and one local band didn't show up, so after Grady finished his gig, he went over to the other stage and, without a break, filled in for the other act.

Grady had started playing at a club called Spirits in Alexandria. I had done a psychohistory of Otis Redding, and the (US) Postal Service issued a postage stamp featuring Otis that I helped to fund. To commemorate the unveiling of the stamp, we did a show at Spirits. I had not met Patrick Harris, but my fiancée had seen him in another band and told me how good he was. I said, "That band's not very good," and she said, "I'm not talking about the band. I'm talking about Patrick, and you've got to introduce him to Grady." That night at the postal party, Patrick dropped in and did three songs with Grady, and that's how they met. Grady renamed him "Mr. Excitement."

This was around the time that Paul and Big Robert had got in a huge fight one night when the band was playing at a club. I mean, it was a big fight. They tore the place up pretty bad. I actually wasn't there that night. I was in Louisiana, so it was good that my name wasn't attached to it. I had to fire 'em both after that. But while they were out, I heard about this singer named Patrick Harris, and he got up and sang with us at Spirits. From the moment I first heard him sing, I knew I'd found the vocalist I'd been looking for. The night I first met him, he sang "Knock on Wood" and "Mustang Sally," and I said, "That's the one for me."

Patrick Harris

I WAS PLAYING A GIG with a band named Chameleon at Spirits when Greg Gormanous saw me and told Grady about me. When I met Greg, he told me Grady was coming through here from Tipitina's in New Orleans and said I ought to come back here next week to meet him. He told me the rundown on Grady—that he played with Little Richard and all that history, so I came back, and he let me sit in with him, and I've been with him ever since. It's about twenty years or so now. I was real excited to hear about his history because a lot of those guys were my heroes. I've always been into old-school music. My father played guitar and sang Muddy Waters, Howlin' Wolf, and all that, so I grew up around it. After I met Grady, it gave me the opportunity to get deeper into that stuff since the band was playing a whole lot of blues then. Me and Grady just clicked right away.

I remember while we were recording *Horn of Plenty* in New Orleans, we had a gig scheduled at city hall in Alexandria (Louisiana). I was concentrating so hard in the studio that I didn't think about that we had to play that night in Alexandria. Greg called me from Alexandria while I was in the middle of recording a tune, and I said, "God damn!" I thought I was gonna miss that gig, so I got on the phone and called Big Robert and told him to call Nell and for her to give him the keys to the van, and I told Robert to call all the musicians and hightail it to Alexandria.

Greg Gormanous

GRADY HAD BEEN UP ALL NIGHT, and Hammond drove him to Baton Rouge. They told me they ate some shish kabobs or something on the way. I picked up Grady in Baton Rouge and drove him to Alexandria. Grady slept about forty-five minutes in the car and did the gig. I remember he didn't take a break during that gig because there were about three hundred people there, and he knew if he took a break, they'd lose the crowd. So they played straight through, packed up the equipment, and drove back to Houston that night for the picture session for *Horn of Plenty* the next day. He basically went two days without sleep.

Nell Pharms

I STARTED GOING EVERYWHERE they'd play, and that's how I met Little Richard. They were playing at the Long Beach Blues Festival (1996) when I saw Little Richard and yelled, "Hey, Little Richard. I'm Nell, Grady's girlfriend." He was getting into his limo, and I told him to come over to Roy's club (Gainesville USA in Los Angeles) for the after-party. I told Grady I'd invited Little Richard, and he said he was going to come, but Grady didn't believe he'd make it. But he did come and had a good time.

Keyboardist Teddy Reynolds, Little Richard, and Grady around the time of the Long Beach Jazz Festival, 1996. Photo from the Grady Gaines Collection.

Greg Gormanous

EVERY YEAR, the (Long Beach Blues) festival features something special, and the year Grady came out they did a Duke/ Peacock (Records) tribute. They billed it as a Grady Gaines and Little Richard reunion. The emcee said something like, "History talks about Little Richard being the black Elvis, but it's just the opposite. Elvis is the white Little Richard!" Before his show, Little Richard told me he would put a chair next to his piano and when he gave me the signal, I would help Grady up on the chair so he could get up on top of the piano. It was during the third song, "Good Golly, Miss Molly," and when I brought Grady up, he forgot about his arthritis and that he was sixty-something years old and sprinted out there, stepped one foot on the chair, and got on top of the piano. The nineteen or twenty thou-

Roy Gaines and Grady in the early '90s. Photo from the Grady Gaines Collection.

sand people in the crowd went berserk. That was a chill-bump moment for me. When I get to heaven and St. Peter won't let me in, at least I got that as a trump card!

That night, we got a nice car for me, Carol Fran, Grady, Nell, and (former Peacock Records arranger/talent scout) Joe Scott's widow and son, and we rode out to Gainesville USA. We were riding around, talking about the old days. Joe Scott's son must have been around twenty-two or so. His daddy died when he was young, and he didn't know who his daddy was, really. At the club, people would come up to him and say, "You're Joe Scott's son? Let me tell you about your father," and they would start telling stories. I think he was into rap, but he got up and played drums to some blues, and he found himself that night at Gainesville USA.

Roy owned Gainesville USA for a good long while. It was a record-ing studio and nightclub located on Crenshaw Street in Los Angeles, and a lot of people played there, like Lowell Fulson, Tyrone Davis, and Clarence Holliman. I had the idea of having the after-party at the club, and it was jam-packed. Richard didn't play; he just did his thing, like meeting and greeting the people. Richard had called me and told me he wanted me to put all the old band members together to play behind him at the festival, and everything went super.

CHAPTER 12

Still Blowin'

After I hired Patrick (Harris), we started practicing from ten in the morning until ten at night most days. See, Patrick would listen to me and do what I asked him to do. That's why he became as good a vocalist as he is now. Most vocalists I hire, whether it's a male or female, don't want to listen. They feel like they know already.

We was working six, seven nights a week at this time, and one of the places we played a lot was a club called Evening Shadows. Mrs. Vonell Johnson was the owner, and she was crazy about our group. I would play the shit out of "Something on Your Mind," and Patrick would sing "It Don't Hurt No More" by Buddy Ace, and women would run him all around the stage trying to get to him. He was dynamite. He actually stayed in my house, lived in the back room, for about five years when he moved here from Louisiana. I would try to teach him everything I knew, so now he's dynamite on that stage. I mean, he tears down the house everywhere we go.

Paul and Big Robert were out of the band at this time after the fight, but both wanted to come back in. They started hearing about Patrick and started coming to Evening Shadows to check him out. One night Paul said to me, "Man, you sure know how to pick 'em." I eventually did let Paul and Big Robert back in, so now I had three male vocalists and Earlie Huntsberry as the female vocalist. I would have to space them all out during a show by bringing Paul on first, then Big Robert, then Earlie between Robert and Patrick. We had a real balanced show, and the band was cookin'. Joe James was a guitar player I had in the band around this time, and he could play and sing, too. He would stand on his head, hang out of a tree upside down, and play with his legs wrapped around a tree. He was a real showman.

Patrick Harris, Texas Upsetters vocalist

THE FIRST GIG I PLAYED with Grady was at the Houston Music Awards (actually the 1993 Houston Juneteenth Festival, where Gaines was named Blues Artist of the Year). Nobody knew it was my first gig because I just fit right in like I was supposed to be there. Me and Grady just seem to have a lot in common. People would ask me, "How can y'all have a lot in common with such an age difference?" But I guess I'm an old soul, and I have a deep love for that music and that time and what those guys went through. They did music for real. No drum machines, harmony boxes, or effects; either you could play or you couldn't. You had to make people feel something with your instrument or your voice, and any mistakes you made, people heard them.

Throughout the 1990s, Grady Gaines and the Texas Upsetters were a well-oiled machine and one of the most popular party bands in the Houston area. Private parties, many of them held in homes and country club ballrooms located in some of Houston's toniest neighborhoods, like River Oaks, Memorial, and Tanglewilde, became the band's bread and butter. As Gaines celebrated five decades in the music business, he began to receive long-overdue recognition for his impact on the genres of blues and rhythm and blues. He received the Blues Heritage Award from the Blues Preservation Society, which hailed him as a "Texas blues ambassador around the world and a pioneer in the creation of rock 'n' roll." In 1990 the band appeared on the bill at high-profile events such as the 1990 inauguration of Texas governor Ann Richards. In 1993 he was named the Blues Artist of the Year at the Houston Juneteenth Festival, but the year was also marked by the first serious health scare of Grady's life. After feeling faint while at home, he was taken by ambulance to a nearby hospital, where it was determined that he had suffered a mild heart attack at age fifty-nine. Gaines was forced to take nearly a month off from performing to recuperate and was prescribed heart medication, which he still takes daily.

In 1994 Grady served as the grand marshal of the inaugural Alexandria (Louisiana) Mardi Gras parade. But the highlight of 1994 occurred when Grady Gaines and the Texas Upsetters were chosen to be the featured attraction at the Texas party for President Bill Clinton's second inauguration. The event, held at the Mayflower Hotel in Washington, DC, was attended by several hundred people. Houston musicians Clarence Holliman and Carol Fran also performed with the Texas Upsetters.

That (inaugural party) was one of the best nights of my musical career. We really got over big that night. Unfortunately, Clinton didn't have his sax with him, but he waved and gave us a thumbs up. The gig we played at the Houston Juneteenth Festival, where I was named blues artist of the year, was also a memorable show. It was at Miller Outdoor Theatre (an amphitheater located in Hermann Park, which features a large, grassy, spectator hill), and we tore the house up! I walked all through the crowd and up on the hill, and there was a line of people following me around.

Grady setting up to play at President Bill Clinton's second inauguration in 1993. He's sporting the wig he wore for a brief period at the time. Photo from the Grady Gaines Collection.

Jump Start (Gulf Coast Records, 2002) was recorded at Houston's Eighth Note Productions studios and was produced by Grady and Susan Criner for her husband's label, Gulf Coast Records. Featuring fewer original songs and songs written by members of the band than Gaines's previous studio release, it focuses on older songs given fresh arrangements by Gaines and the Texas Upsetters. Of the eleven tracks on the album, only two instrumentals, "KP" and the disc's final piece, "Flip Flop," are originals, with both crediting Gaines as the writer. Susan Criner commented that the intent was for Grady to do material that was different from what he had recorded with Black Top. Great care was taken to select cover songs that were somewhat unique and would appeal to the private party and festival markets. The album features contributions from many of the musicians who make up the current lineup of the Texas Upsetters, including Patrick Harris, Grady Gaines Jr. (soprano sax), Paul David Roberts (trombone and vocals), Wayne Richards (bass), and Yvette Busby (vocals). It marks the final recorded appearance for Big Robert Smith as a member of the Texas Upsetters, as the burly singer would die in 2006 at age sixty-six.

Jump Start also benefits from the contributions of trumpet player and arranger Nelson Mills III. A Houston native, Mills attended Houston's Texas Southern University, where he was a member of the legendary 1960s' and '70s' soul group the TSU Toronados, who achieved fame in 1968 as the backing band on the megasmash "Tighten Up" by Archie Bell and the Drells. Mills, who spent several years contributing stellar trumpet playing and arrangements as a member of blues, jazz, and R&B legend Calvin Owens's band, joined the Texas Upsetters in 2000. He played a key role in crafting the sophisticated, tasteful, and funky horn-section arrangements that permeate *Jump Start*. In addition to his continued work with the Texas Upsetters, he is also a member of "200 Mondays," a Houston Jazz group.

Nelson Mills, Texas Upsetters trumpet player/arranger

I HAD BEEN with Calvin Owens' band for a long time but asked out of the band to pursue some other things, including writing for some people around town. Grady was looking for a trumpet player and asked Calvin if he knew anybody, and he recommended me. I joined Grady's band in October 2000, but my wife (Houston blues and R&B singer Gloria Edwards) went to Singapore and asked me to play piano for her, but when we came back a year later, I rejoined Grady and have been with him since.

I used to see Grady playing in the clubs when I was a kid. All of us kids in our teens and twenties knew about Grady, but we were more impressed that he played with Sam Cooke than with Little Richard because that's who we grew up with. To me, Grady was the essence of cool because you hardly ever saw him coming to a place or walking down the street when he didn't have a suit on. And he had that straight-up walk that made it seem like he damn near ruled the world. He wore some of the most beautiful suits I've ever seen, but it wasn't like flamboyancy; he was just cool like that. Every time I saw him I thought, "Now that is what an old musician is supposed to look like."

In the Texas Upsetters, we've got some older guys like Jim Fawn (trumpet) and, no disrespect to Jim—because I love him—but he's about ten years older than me, and his thing is big-band jazz music. I love that, too, but I came up with Motown. Him and Grady came up when horns played whole notes for background, but me and Paul (David Roberts) came up when horns played dat-a-tat-tat-dat-a-tat-tat, you know, sixteenth notes. So once we integrated that to fit today's times, it took the horn section to another level.

On the *Jump Start* sessions, my role was to upgrade the horns because these were some old songs. I had to try to do something to make 'em fresh and more up to date. When Grady first gave me the tape to start listening to those songs to see what we were gonna do to 'em, I brought it home, turned it on, and thought, "What can we do to this stuff?" They sounded like 1950s' and

'60s' songs, so were we gonna just do them over or try to do something to it, and I got the understanding from Grady to do what we could with 'em to make 'em fresh.

Like on the Little Richard song ("Hey, Hey, Hey, Hey") that Patrick sang, we updated the chord structure, and the horns played some real nice closed-in chords that made it sound even bigger than it was. I also have to credit Wayne Richards, the bass player, with producing some really great rhythm work. With him doing the rhythm work, when we started working on that stuff together and started punching those horns on top, it really popped. Even my wife thought *Jump Start* was pretty entertaining, and she knows music and is pretty hard on people.

One thing I've always believed in is I've got to have real strong singers in the band. All of the singers I've had have to have some showmanship and be able to sing a variety of music. Usually, when they'd come in here, they don't know what to do, and they feel like what they been doing was all right, but when you step into this band, you got a different way of doing everything. You might do it your way, but you don't do it the way we do it. The way we do it, you can tear it up.

Recording with Grady Jr. was really nice, too, and he's a hell of a horn player. We've played quite a few gigs together now. He's better than I am at taking a horn and playing a whole set solo with just him and no other musicians, plus he can play all the reed instruments, and that makes me real proud of him. He did a solo on "Let Them Talk" on *Jump Start*. Grady Jr. is the only one of my kids that went into music, and now one of his sons is in college and playing music. When he's not playing with his band, he makes some gigs with my band.

Not just anybody can play all the private parties, weddings, and gigs at these country club–type places where we mostly play now because you have to be able to read the crowd. But the band I had a few years ago was more like a family, and we all stuck together. Whatever I wanted, they all tried to make it happen. This band I got now, I have to go through different sources to make happen what I want to happen. It just be so much harder doing it that way, but I get the job done.

Grady and Milton Hopkins, 2001. Photo courtesy of the Milton Hopkins Collection.

Robert "Little Robert" Lewis

IF A MUSICIAN hit that stage and didn't have their tie and suit straight, they'd get a fine for sure. You had to be clean and all the way tight, but Grady also always looked after the band and didn't let nobody come on stage and pick at you or anything. We traveled in a blue 1970s' model van with a trailer on the back with "Grady Gaines and the Texas Upsetters" painted on it, and I drove most of the time. But a few times we hit the road, and I might have had too much to drink, and Grady would look at me and ask, "Little Robert, you all right?" and I'd say, "No sir." Grady would go ahead and take the wheel and never pushed the issue. And Grady owned one of just about every instrument in the band, so if somebody forgot theirs, we'd have another one. But he didn't trust nobody to be on time for a gig, so we picked every band member up, and when we came back in, we'd drop 'em off one at a time, and sometimes there'd be as many as twelve people in the band. If we had a gig at seven, we'd be there at one o'clock, you can believe that. He didn't believe in being late, so sometimes you'd have to sit in the van and wait. If you had to go cool off or get something to eat, he didn't mind paying for it.

The band I got now, they don't understand nothing like that (being picked up to avoid anyone being late to a gig). They don't know what kind of pains I had to go through for them to be able to get paid the way they get paid now. See, they ain't paid none of they dues, and they walked in on a good thing. Now that's a fact. And do they appreciate it? From my standpoint, hell no! I have to go through all kind of changes. I mean, you got something that you know works, and it has always worked for you, and you bring it up, and the band I got now wants to change it. They're good musicians, but it seems like they have one way of doing music and don't want to do it no other way. So I ask myself, "What should I do to make them understand?" But I say, as long as they do what I want on my jobs onstage, I'm OK. We been together fifteen, twenty years, and I've been dealing with it that long. I just feel like we have a strange way of loving each other.

Paul David Roberts

GRADY KNOWS EVERYTHING from A to Z about the entertainment business. That's the first thing I tell people that he hires: You can't pull no tricks on Grady. He doesn't say anything, and he'll let you run your course, but when he says something to you, it's time for you to make the decision whether you're gonna do it his way or hit the highway. I warn everybody to just make your money because Grady knows what he's doing. But if you make him upset, if you do something contrary to his plan, he'll say something. And you got two choices: Either change or go find you work someplace else. But it's worked for us for all this time, and they don't know the price that Grady had to pay. It wasn't easy, man. Me and Grady disagree on certain things, but I always ended up doing what he said because I learned that what he was saying was right. Man, we've got a song book with over five hundred songs in it! In the beginning, I was one of the most ridiculous people in the band, but I had to learn because I was learning from him, and he don't let nothing interfere with his business. I remember one night we were playing a gig, and the electricity went off, and I went out and cut limbs off a tree and played drums on a bucket, but we made the gig. Grady taught me not to let anything keep you from making your money, so I learned to listen to him because he was teaching me about life and everything imaginable. I try to settle Grady down because I had a stroke, and I know what it'll do to you when you get stressed. So I talk to Grady and tell him not to get stressed because if something happens to Grady, it folds. I tell him he'll make himself sick worried about bullshit.

These people walk into a band that's working four and five nights a week, and they always got something negative to say and second-guess what I'm doing. I tell 'em, "What you did over there, you do it over there, but when you in here with Grady, you do it the way I want it." You have bandleaders from other bands come and watch us play, and if you go to one of their gigs, you'll see them trying to do the same thing we did—same songs, same routines. The ones that be doing all this talking in my band now, I mean, you wouldn't believe it. They doing all the talking, but they stayed in the band; some of them been in there fifteen, sixteen, seventeen years, and they doing all that stupid-ass talking. It pisses me off, and they don't know how that eats me up. They don't know what I feel like doing, but I'm just not that type of person. I don't really fire people in the band. I warn them three or four times, then whoever that person is, I tell them, "I think I'm going to try something different." That's the way all the members of my band would leave the band. That's why I say I don't fire anybody; they fire themselves. I feel comfortable doing it that way because, you see, I'm a person that hates to get rid of anyone.

I refuse to fight anybody. When I fight somebody, it's just nothing else I can do but maybe lay them off a week or two. But I just hate to fight about it, and that's my way of thinking, and I've been that way my whole life. Even when I was at the hotels when I was transportation manager, I was over all those guys, and I could fire whoever I wanted to fire, but I always gave them all kinds of chances.

Reginald Yarborough, Texas Upsetters drummer and stage manager since 1998

THIS IS THE ONLY BAND I know where you fire yourself. He won't fire you; you fire yourself. I'm like the guy in the middle. I hear what Grady wants and hear their (band members') complaints. What I do is sugarcoat what Grady's saying for them because Grady is straight to the point, and if you don't know him, sometimes you might take it the wrong way because he is strictly about business. I've learned the business side and the side of learning how to talk to these musicians in a different way where I get the point across. If they don't get it, I'm angry, and he'll get mad at me because I didn't do my job. I say, "The man has spoken. This is what he wants, and this is what you've got to do. If you don't do it this way, then it's out of my hands. I have to do my job to keep my job, and I'm not gonna lose my job." But I've seen him with musicians who have given him so much problems, but he never disrespects them, never cussed 'em out, and never fires 'em. But they've got to realize that the marquee says, "Grady Gaines and the Texas Upsetters." It's his band, his rules.

When Reggie Yarborough came into the band, he took a lot of weight off of me. He's the drummer, but he's like the road manager and the stage manager. He hired an assistant stage manager, Thomas Davis, to help him out. Now he's like my right-hand man.

With these musicians now, it's as simple as if I want to do a number or if the client told the office they want this song played, but they (the musicians) don't like the number, (and) they don't want to do it. But that can't happen, and they're gonna have to play it. But they disagree with that, and that's how stupid they can be. I don't understand how people who are supposed to be college educated and got all kinds of degrees can be so stupid. They ain't got good common sense. It's simple. I tell 'em how it goes because I've got the guidelines that I have to go by, and if I don't go by 'em, there ain't gonna be no job. Period. They think it ought to be what they think it ought to be, but it ain't gonna go that way. It never went that way, and it never will go that way as long as I'm in charge. I don't have to name no names. They know who they are, and when they see it in the book, they will easily know because I'm putting it in the exact words about the ones that do this stuff.

Susan Criner

I DON'T KNOW HOW Grady leads that band. I've watched the personnel for over twenty years, and it's amazing how stable it is. He's had crackheads in the band and dealt with every kind of issue and somehow manages to keep the peace. With a band that's working only once a week and doesn't tour, it's hard to make payroll, but he runs it like a business. I don't get involved in how he pays out the members, but he has to deal with a lot of personalities.

Nelson Mills III

I KNOW WHAT IT'S LIKE to be a (band)leader, so I don't mind being a follower because I don't want to pay the cost to be a leader. I've been one before, and it's hard work. Me and my wife had a band in Kansas City when we lived there, and it was one of the best bands around at the time. But it was such a hassle because when you're a bandleader, band members come to you and want you to keep their children for 'em, or you have to be a

marriage counselor and stuff like that. You don't just deal with
the music, load up your car, and go home. Long after you been at
home, some wife comes knocking at your door at three o'clock in
the morning going, "Have you seen my husband?"

Reginald Yarborough

THE BIG DIFFERENCE I SEE is that me and Grady do this for a
living; it's how we pay our bills. I only recently got a day job, but
the other musicians have jobs, so they don't take it as serious as
we do. When you depend on this to pay all your bills, you respect
it much more. When you don't, you respect it less, but just look
at the money you're making. The average musician in Houston
is not making this kind of money, so just listen and enjoy the
income. Some musicians say, "I don't think this is right." But
he didn't ask for your opinion. He's asked you to do this. Now,
Grady does have his mean side if you get him to that point, and if
he calls a meeting, look out! But there's no bandleader as honest
as Grady is. A lot of bandleaders say one thing and do another.
This man, whatever it comes down to, he's gonna split it right
down the middle. He does think about his band. When people
give tips, he splits it down the middle. Other bandleaders put it
in their pocket.

We played a wedding not too long ago over in Beaumont, and this lady
wrote to Susan's office that our band was so great that we made the party.
She said even her eighty-nine- or ninety-year-old grandfather was out
on the dance floor, and that tells you a whole lot. I got a whole bunch
of these (thank-you letters). Every time I get a letter after a gig I put it
in here (a manila folder), and some of the things people say are the best
things you could hear about a band. Playing the parties is good money,
and they take care of you. I could be out there playing the clubs, but I've
got a big band, and I can't pay them on what the clubs are paying.

Patrick Harris

GRADY DID WHAT HE NEEDED to do to get into these places (upscale venues) because taking an all-black band into these places, it's not gonna happen unless you know somebody or have some credibility. The only way to get into those places is to play the music the people want to hear, and he knew exactly the kind of music we needed to play, so all he had to do was get the musicians and the vocalists he needed so we could start playing more Sinatra, Tony Bennett, Sammy Davis Jr., the Platters, Temptations, Four Tops, Ink Spots, Etta James, Righteous Brothers, and stuff like that.

With my band now, it's a show within the band itself because everybody sings. I got two girl singers (Yvette Busby and Cynthia Antoine, and the whole horn section (Paul David Roberts, Jim Fawn, Nelson Mills III) sings, plus the guitar player (Rick Restelli) sings. My band now also includes Reggie Yarborough on drums, John Hernandez on keyboards, and Wayne Richards on bass, and Larry Garza is our sound man. Plus Grady Jr. plays a lot of gigs with us. When you hire my band, you're hiring the whole show, and we don't do the same thing all night; it all depends on what kind of crowd we're playing for. Some crowds really want you to mix it up and not do too much of one thing or they get tired. So we put something new on 'em so they get a different feeling, and the band gets off on that, too. We've proved it so many times that I've gotten to know what to put on 'em, and that comes from all the experience I've had from all the acts I've played behind.

Susan Criner

WHEN WE BOOK the Texas Upsetters to play a private party, we always ask for ideal conditions for the band, including a proper stage, dressing rooms, and a hot meal for the band. We don't want any surprises when they show up. They have to be well

Grady at Houston Metro bus stop featuring photos of himself and other prominent Third Ward musicians, 2013. Photo by Rod Evans.

taken care of. Grady is the most accommodating bandleader I've ever seen. There's never anything that's too much trouble for him to do for the client, whether it's acting as an emcee, playing without a break, learning new songs, talking to the client, or, God forbid, letting the client come on stage and sing with him. In the beginning, the Upsetters played about thirty to fifty gigs a year. I guess the heyday was 2007 to 2009, which was the heyday for everybody in this business in Houston. Back then, I think they played about sixty gigs a year. In 2013 they played about thirty-eight to forty gigs. The market for Grady won't go away because it's the high-end, private-party market. The only issue for Grady is keeping up with current material. Lots of brides want Top 40 music, and that's not his strong suit. But they add about a half a dozen new songs a year (to the playlist).

The girls and Patrick can sing any of the new stuff, so we're able to do anything we need to do for any crowd we play for. Every decade, music and music styles change, so I had to have different singers, and if I didn't have somebody who could do what I needed, I'd have to go out and get somebody to put in there along with what I got. I have to make sure I have what I need to do what I want to do. I never did do what other bands around here or around other places do—never did and I still don't. I've never wanted to be one of them bands like when you hear one, you've heard 'em all. That ain't me.

Of course, we gotta practice to learn all these songs, but I got good musicians, and that helps a lot. What I do when we gotta learn new songs is I make a CD or tape and give it to the rhythm section. Nelson Mills helps with the music, and Wayne Richards (bassist) helps with the music, too. They have a few days to listen to the CDs; then we rehearse. When we play a wedding or something, if load-in is at four o'clock, we might set up so we have time to learn the songs and get familiar with them. Sometimes we have to take more time.

Patrick Harris

WE WERE PLAYING A BIG OUTDOOR SHOW in Lafayette (Louisiana), and I don't know how it happened, but some kind of way, some girl grabbed my shoes and took 'em off my feet. I never did get those shoes back. As part of the show, I was laying down on my back on the stage, and she just took 'em. I had to finish the show in just my socks! I used to wear these blood-red socks and a red tuxedo shirt and black and red vest. Why? I don't know. It just fit what I was doing at the time. Grady wore a lot of wild stuff, so that's where that came from, I guess. I was trying to keep up with him. I remember another time we did a one-nighter in Belgium. We did the show and flew back the next morning. Junior Wells was on that show, along with a bunch of other people. Once we got back to Houston, we had to get ready to do another show that night, but I loved it. Being younger, I never would get tired, and I'd ask the other band members, "Why are y'all tired?" Now that I've gotten older, I understand a little better.

One good memory I have from a wedding gig is the night (country singer) Clay Walker came in when we were playing a reception at the Woodlands Country Club. He performed with us the whole night, and I thought he would sing country, but he sang R&B all night—stuff like "Brick House."

But I'll never forget we were playing at the Long Beach Blues Festival (1996) with Little Richard. Roy (Gaines), "Guitar Shorty" (David Kearney), and Jimmy "T-99" Nelson were there, too. Well, Grady jumped up on Richard's piano and was doing all that stuff he does, and Richard broke the band down and said, "Hold on, Grady! This is my show!" He don't like you to upstage him.

Paul David Roberts

WE WERE PLAYING at Rockefeller's, and I was thinking about Muddy Waters, but we were backing up Bo Diddley, so I gave him this big buildup and said, "Ladies and gentlemen, here's Muddy Waters!" When he came on stage, he cursed me out! There was another time when we were playing at the opening of the Aquarium (a downtown Houston restaurant that houses an expansive aquarium), and Chris (Perry), our drummer, spotted Clint Black (country singer from Houston) in the crowd, but there was another country singer there, a guy from Beaumont (Clay Walker) in the crowd, too. Well, Chris gave a shout-out to Clint Black, but he called him by the other's guy's (Walker's) name, so Clint Black got pissed off and left. Another incident that happened when the mayor (Houston mayor Annise Parker, the first openly gay mayor of a major US city) was dancing with her partner. I was singing "If Loving You Is Wrong," and I had a little monologue on it where I said, "Whomever you love is all right with me," and the mayor threw a sign at me, and we both laughed because she knew what I was referring to.

On February 29, 2012, Grady Gaines and the Texas Upsetters head-lined the "Preserving a Legacy: A Tribute to Houston Blues" con-cert at Jones Hall, the venerable venue in downtown Houston, usually reserved for symphony and opera performances. The concert, which drew more than twenty-one hundred people, was part of a monthlong project organized by the Society for the Performing Arts (SPA). With photo exhibits and numerous performances by Houston area musicians, the project celebrated the distinctive style of blues that developed in the city's Third and Fifth Wards from the end of World War II up to the mid-1970s. The concert was the crowning touch on the celebration. In addition to the Texas Upsetters, the lineup that night included Grady's longtime friend and colleague Milton Hopkins, guitarist Texas Johnny Brown, who passed away at age eighty-five in July 2013, singers Trudy Lynn and Ray Brown, and the Kashmere Reunion Stage Band.

The Texas Upsetters served as the house band for the night, open-ing the show with their own three-song set and playing behind each of the featured singers. Grady was in fine form despite suffering from the effects of the flu, and dressed in full regalia, including a flowing, purple sequined cape. As the musical director for the revue-style show, Gaines worked with each artist in selecting the songs they would perform. Observers say the concert was the first blues show ever held at Jones Hall.

Susan told me about the date at Jones Hall and said our band would do a set and play behind all of the other acts, so I put everything together. That included our opening number and then putting the acts where I felt like they could get the most of what they were doing. But I caught the flu and was sick on the day of the concert. But I told Susan, "Don't worry. I've played sick before."

After Susan gave me the names of the people on the show, I called them to figure out what songs they would do. I called Milton Hopkins first, and he left it up to me, so I said, "You come over to the house and bring your guitar." He said he wanted to do "Honky Tonk" and Gatemouth Brown's "Okie Dokie Stomp." Because Milton's a cousin of

Grady Gaines and the Texas Upsetters, 2013: front row (left to right), Grady Gaines Jr. (saxophone), Patrick Harris (vocals), Yvette Busby (vocals), Grady Gaines, Cynthia Antoine (vocals), Jim Fawn (trumpet); back row (left to right), Wayne Richards (bass), Thomas Davis (assistant stage manager), Paul David Roberts (trombone, vocals), John Hernandez (keyboards), Larry Garza (sound), Rick Restelli (guitar), Nelson Mills III (trumpet), Reginald Yarborough (drums, stage manager). Photo courtesy Ioman Imagery.

Lightnin' Hopkins, we had to figure out a way to get some Lightnin' Hopkins in there since people expect him to do some Lightnin'. So we took a couple of verses out of one of Lightnin's biggest songs and did a little of that before we did the last song, "Dust My Broom" by Elmore James.

Texas Johnny Brown was the next one I talked to, and I asked him over the phone what songs he wanted to do. I told him to send me two songs, but we'll need three in case you get called back to the stage. I called Trudy Lynn next and did the same with her before I called up Ray Brown, who wanted to do a James Brown song ("I Feel Good") and a hip-hop tune. All of the acts got called back for one more song, so we had to play the chaser to keep everything on time. My band played "Something on Your Mind" to close our part of the show, and the people went stone wild.

It was a lot of brainish work putting that show together. It wasn't too hard on one hand, but it was on another because we were in the midst of learning some songs for weddings and parties, and then I messed around and got the flu and was sick as a dog on the day of the show.

Greg Gormanous

GRADY'S IMPACT IN MUSIC is amazing, really. I was flying into San Francisco one night and sat next to Clarence Clemons (the late saxophonist with Bruce Springsteen and the E Street Band). We got to talking, and I said, "I don't know if you know a buddy of mine named Grady Gaines?" He stopped me and said, "Everybody in music knows Grady Gaines." About a year later I was in Paris searching out old CDs, and I was looking for copies of the *Live at Tipitina's* CD. I walked into a little music store and told the man, "I'm looking for something you've probably never heard of by a sax player named Grady Gaines," and he stopped me and said, "Sir, everybody knows who Grady Gaines is."

Grady has played with and backed more people currently in the Rock and Roll Hall of Fame than anybody to my knowledge. The Hall of Fame inducted Little Walter (in 2008) as a sideman because he helped make the harmonica be looked at as an instrument. Grady has made the sax that kind of driving instrument, but he was always a sideman and never wanted the spotlight. It was about the music and who he was backing.

Determining whether Gaines has played with more Rock and Roll Hall of Fame inductees than anyone in history is a difficult task. By Grady's own count he and his bands have backed seventy-one acts inducted into the Hall of Fame onstage or in the studio. Here's the list:

Little Richard	Jackie Wilson	The Moonglows
Sam Cooke	The Supremes	Solomon Burke
James Brown	Bobby "Blue" Bland	Bobby Womack
Fats Domino	Etta James	The Coasters
Bo Diddley	Gladys Knight and the Pips	Eddie Cochran
B. B. King	Little Willie John	Aretha Franklin
T-Bone Walker	Curtis Mayfield	Carl Perkins
Smokey Robinson	Big Joe Turner	The Drifters
Dion	Otis Redding	Soul Stirrers
The Temptations	Hank Ballard	Bobby Darin
The Four Seasons	The Four Tops	The Platters
LaVern Baker	John Lee Hooker	The Impressions
Wilson Pickett	Jimmy Reed	Ike and Tina Turner
Booker T and the MGs	Isley Brothers	Sam and Dave
Ruth Brown	Frankie Lymon and the Teenagers	Willie Dixon
Duane Eddy	Johnny Otis	Martha and the Vandelas
The Orioles	The Shirelles	Lloyd Price
Allen Toussaint	Gene Vincent	Charles Brown
Del Shannon	The Staple Singers	King Curtis
The Flamingos	Richie Valens	Brenda Lee
The Righteous Brothers	The Dells	Buddy Guy
The O'Jays	Percy Sledge	The Ronettes
The Ventures	Little Anthony and the Imperials	Freddie King
The Midnighters	The Miracles	

I'm not going to be out there killing myself like I used to with a three- or four-piece band. My wind ain't what it used to be when I was fifty-eight. By doing things this way I can prolong my life and my music. I got these other horn players to help me, so I don't have to blow so hard. There was a time when I could take that one horn and tear it up just as much as we do with these other horns. But you have to have good common sense. That's why I've lasted over six decades in the music business. When you get to where I am in life now, you have to take it easy so the world can still enjoy my musical talents. Me and Nell have a real good life, and I want to be strong enough to play my sax.

Hammond Scott

THE FIRST TIME I WENT TO GRADY'S HOUSE, I was impressed that he was a good saver and had something to show for his career, which is the nice home he had built. I was also impressed that he had someone like Nell with him. For as long as I've known Grady, Nell has been there to provide that kind of consistency in his life.

I was struck by a story about Grady and Roy Gaines told to me by a guy who'd worked at a music store in Houston (possibly H&H Music) for a long time. He told me that the Gaines brothers were "raised well and had a lot of responsibility about them," and that's definitely true. But you can see how successful Grady has been in ways that you may not notice at first, like when he whips out a credit card, and he might have a little higher level (credit limit), and that speaks to his responsibility, organizational skills, and business skills.

It's a real blessing to still be around playing music and being able to tell my story. I tell young kids coming through school who are into music and want to be a bandleader that you can expect lots of ups and downs, but you got to keep your head on straight, your body strong, and think with your brain and not your heart. You run into all different kinds of personalities, so you have to be careful how you express yourself when someone

Grady and Nell at home, 2014. Photo by Rod Evans.

(in your band) rebels at you. You have to be careful how you talk to them. I always say I'll take the low road, and I've come out all right. But when you take the low road, you'll take a lot of stuff that you don't particularly like and that you know is wrong, but with the strength from God, you'll be able to accept what band members are dishing out to you.

You can be ever so good to them, but that don't mean they'll return the favor. There's always two or three of them that will give you all kinds of hell, but when they give you that hell, smile with 'em, keep your chin up, and say "God forgive 'em" and "We'll get through this." When they (band members) give me all that hell and cause all that stress, to relax my mind and relieve the stress they've given me, I tell 'em, "You can treat me mean, but I'll keep on loving you just the same." That means I forgive them.

Notes

Chapter 3

1. Some of the biographical information in this chapter is courtesy of Allmusic.com. http://www.allmusic.com/artist/louis-jordan-mn0000287604/biography, accessed July 13, 2013.

2. Adapted from Owens's obituary by Andrew Dansby, *Houston Chronicle,* February 20, 2008.

Chapter 4

1. Article text from cover image courtesy of Flickr.com. http://www.flickr.com/photos/vieilles_annonces/3655162626/in/set-72157602208125140/, accessed September 18, 2013.

Chapter 5

1. A portion of Robey's biographical information was adapted from *Down in Houston: Bayou City Blues* (Austin: University of Texas Press, 2003), a book by Roger Wood, with photography by James Fraher.

Chapter 7

1. Cast information courtesy of IMDb.com. *The Girl Can't Help It:* http://www.imdb.com/title/tt0049263/?ref_=nv_sr_1; *Don't Knock the Rock:* http://www.imdb.com/title/tt0049152/?ref_=fn_al_tt_1; *Mr. Rock 'n' Roll:* http://www.imdb.com/title/tt0050711/, accessed July 24, 2013.

Chapter 8

1. Some of the information here is adapted from *The Life and Times of Little Richard: The Authorised Biography* (London: Omnibus Press, 1984), by Charles White.

2. Biographical information courtesy of Allmusic.com. http://www.allmusic.com/artist/dee-clark-mn0000197582/biography, accessed August 6, 2013.

3. Biographical and record chart information courtesy of Allmusic.com. http://www.allmusic.com/artist/little-willie-john-mn0000269972/biography, accessed August 10, 2013.

4. Some of this information comes from *Rolling Stone* magazine 13 (July 1968), 4; and from the *Encyclopedia of Arkansas,* http://www.encyclopediaofarkansas.net/encyclopedia/entry-detail.aspx?search=1&entryID=322, accessed August 10, 2013.

5. Biographical information courtesy of Allmusic.com. http://www.allmusic.com/artist/lc-cook-mn0001457309, accessed September 25, 2012.

6. Song title, label, artist, and songwriter information courtesy of 45-record screenshot on Youtube.com. https://www.youtube.com/watch?v=UxPoEQ4cvuA, accessed September 12, 2012.

7. "Father of Kirbyjon Caldwell Dies at 88," by Cindy George, *Houston Chronicle*, July 17, 2011.

Chapter 9

1. Biographical and record chart information courtesy of Allmusic.com. http://www.allmusic.com/artist/joe-tex-mn0000210323/biography, accessed August 6, 2013.

Chapter 10

1. Information from obituary by Roger Wood, *Houston Chronicle*, April 15, 2006.

2. Biographical information from September 1999 post on Crazy Cajun Music website by John Nova Lomax. http://crazycajunmusic.com/bio-joe-medwick, accessed June 7, 2013.

Chapter 11

1. Information courtesy of Nola.com and CBSnews.com. NOLA.Com: http://www.nola.com/music/index.ssf/2013/02/cheers_to_fats_domino_on_his_8.html, accessed July 25, 2013.

CBSNews.com: http://www.cbsnews.com/news/fats-domino-alive-and-kicking/, accessed July 25, 2013.

Index

ACA Studios, 32, 34
Ace, Buddy, 90
Ace, Johnny, 33, 36, 61
"Aint Gonna Bump No More (With no Big Fat Woman)," 96
Ali, Muhammad (Cassius Clay), 94, 97
Alvis, Eunice, 97
Ammons, Gene, 18, 27, 41, 89
Anchor Room, The, 25, 39
Andrews, John, 90–91, 93, 95, 96
Anson Funderburgh & The Rockets, 113–14, 131
Antoine, Cynthia, 155
Apollo Theater, 44, 48, 82, 90
Arceneaux, Floyd, 22, 90, 108, 122, 126, 131
Archie Bell and the Drells, 146
"At Last," 78

Barnum, H.B., 85–86
Bart, Ben, 85
Beamon, B.B., 85
Bell, Joe, 24, 38
Benton, Brook, 30, 125
Berfect, Sammy, 131
Big Bopper, The, 59
Bill Haley and the Comets, 46
Black, Clint, 158
"Black Night," 19
Black Top Records, 113–14, 122–23, 130–31, 146
Bland, Bobby "Blue," 25, 33–34, 106, 110, 126
Blue Room, The, 90–91

"Blues-a-Rama: Live Down & Dirty," 130, 133, 137
Blues Preservation Society, 144
Blues Ramblers, The, 1, 6, 22, 28, 31, 38–39, 81, 86
Boone, Pat, 6
Bronze Peacock Dinner Club, 30, 33
Brooks, Billy, 39
Brown, Charles, 19, 25, 84
Brown, Clarence "Gatemouth," 24, 33, 36–37, 84, 91, 113, 115, 159
Brown, Nappy, 26
Brown, Ray, 161
Brown, Ruth, 77
Brown, Texas Johnny, 84, 161
Buffalo Booking Agency, 33, 36
Burke, Solomon, 72, 77, 114
Burks, Clifford, 1, 2, 34, 42, 59, 65, 67
Burton, Johnny, 81–82
Busby, Yvette, 146, 155
Butler, Jerry, 72, 106

Caldwell, Booker T., 82, 84
Caldwell Tailors, 81, 84, 102, 120
Calloway, Cab, 81
Carter, Clarence, 109
Champion, Mickey, 28
Charles, Ray, 30, 84, 125
Chenier, Clifton, 26, 84
Chitlin' Circuit, 79–80
City Auditorium, 22, 30, 43
Clark, Dee, 60–63
Clemons, Clarence, 161
Clinton, Jimmy, 59

Clinton, President Bill, 145
Club Delisa, 30, 37
Club Ebony, 37, 90–91, 95
Club Matinee, 24–25, 37, 39, 82, 84, 95
Cobb, Arnett, 18, 41
Cochran, Eddie, 59
"Cold, Cold Feeling," 24
Collins, Albert, 89–90, 106
Connor, Chuck (Charles), 2, 43, 55, 70
Cooke, L.C., 76
Cooke, Sam: Grady on adjusting playing
    style to suit his singing style, 28; on
    Reba Gaines meeting him in Califor-
    nia, 52; and Upsetters backing him,
    70; on tour with Jackie Wilson, 72;
    and fatal shooting, 76; and induction
    into Rock and Roll Hall of Fame, 77;
    Grady meets Cooke's ex-manager, Roy
    Crane, at airport, 92; Roy Gaines on
    "Texas Sound," 125; Hammond Scott
    on "I've Been Out There" recording
    session, 126; Grady on Joe "Guitar"
    Hughes joining band, 133; Nelson
    Mills,III on Grady backing Cooke, 147
Copeland, Johnny, 84, 90
Cosmo's Studio, 133
Crane, Roy, 92
Criner, Susan, 116–17, 146, 153, 155
Crystals, The, 77
Crystal White Cab Co., 14–15, 25
Crystal White Hotel, 25

Diddley, Bo, 72, 77
"Dirty Work at the Crossroads," 36
Dixon, Willie, 128
Dogan, Michael, 90, 108, 124, 128, 135
Domino, Fats, 22, 46, 132–33
"Don't Knock the Rock," 46, 48
Douglas, Nathaniel, 61–62
Down in Houston: Bayou City Blues, 84
Drag Kitchen, 90–91
"Driftin' Blues," 19
Duke, David, 137
Duke's Men's Shop, 82
"Dust My Broom," 161

Eaglin, Snooks, 114
Earl, Ronnie, 114
Eighth Note Productions Studios, 146
Eldorado Ballroom, 37, 40, 84
Elvis (Presley), 6, 48, 55, 59, 140
Emery, Coby, 104, 108
Emery, Etta, 104, 107
Ernest, Herman, 132
Etta's Lounge, 104, 106, 107,104, 112,
    115, 118
Evening Shadows, 143
Everett, Gil, 112

Fawn, Jim, 147, 155
"Fever," 64
Fifth Ward, 14, 16, 33, 81, 84, 90, 94,
    104, 118, 159
Floyd, Eddie, 90
"Flying Home," 22
Forrest, Jimmy, 19
Fran, Carol, 123, 141
Franklin, Bertha, 76
Freed, Alan, 46
"Full Gain," 122–23, 125, 131
Fulson, Lowell, 90–91, 142
"Further on up the Road," 34, 111

Gaines (Carter), Adrena, 9, 12, 79
Gaines, Andy, 9
Gaines, Debra, 78
Gaines, Derrick, 78
Gaines (Harris), Ethel Mae, 11
Gaines, Grady Jr., 21, 58, 78, 100–01,
    146, 148, 155
Gaines, L.C., 9, 12, 20, 52–53
Gaines, Merkerson, 9
Gaines, Merkerson Jr, 9, 12, 14, 17
Gaines, Reba, 9, 52
Gaines, Roy: on his musical inspiration,
    9; on dressing to impress, 15; and
    wanting to play saxophone initially, 17;
    and meeting the Holliman brothers,
    19; L.C. Gaines recalls Grady and Roy
    practicing, 20; and attending Wheatley
    High School, 22; on playing piano in

Grady's band, 24; on being called the "14 year old sensation," 28; playing with T-Bone Walker, 30; recording at Peacock Studios, 32; on visiting California, 52–53; and "Full Gain" sessions, 122–26; and Gainesville USA, 142; Hammond Scott on Gaines brothers, 163

Gaines, Tewanda, 78

Gaines, Van, 78

Gaines, Wanda, 78

Gaines (Hartwell), Wilkie, 9, 79,

Garza, Larry, 155

George, Gorgeous (Theophilus), 67, 80

"Girl Can't Help It, The," 46

Gladys Knight and the Pips, 77

G&M Pleasure Spot, 90, 92, 95

Goffney, Fred, 108

"Good Golly Miss Molly," 140

Gormanous, Greg, 136–37, 140, 161

Grady Gaines Go-Go Girls, 95

Grady Gaines & His All Stars, 90

Grady Gaines & His House Rockers, 22

Grady Gaines & His Orchestra, 90

Grady Gaines & The Crown Jewels, 90

Grady Gaines and The Upsetters, 70, 72, 76, 113

Green, Clarence, 109

Guy, Buddy, 88

Gypsy Tea Room, 37

Hacienda Hotel, 76

H&H Music, 37, 72

Hampton, Lionel, 25, 134

Hank Ballard & The Midnighters, 81

Harlem Music Makers, The, 22

Harris, Elmore, 14–15, 21, 25–26, 79

Harris, Patrick, 138, 143–44, 146, 155, 157

Harris, Sammy, 22

Hartwell, Thomas, 1

"Having a Party," 76

Hendrix, Jimi, 80–81

Hernandez, John, 155

"Hey Little Girl," 61, 63

Hill, Lester, 108

Hinton, Joe, 90, 95

Holiday, Billie, 30, 119, 125

Holliman, Clarence, 19, 22, 122–23, 142, 145

Holliman, Sweets, 19

Hopkins, Lightnin,' 30, 37, 61, 84, 109, 161

Hopkins, Milton, 22, 35, 61–62, 64, 72, 86, 99, 104, 159

Hopper, Dennis, 119

"Horn of Plenty," 131–32, 139

Houston Chronicle, 15, 84

Houston Forward Times, 98

Houston Juneteenth Festival, 144–45

Howard Theater, 51, 78, 90

Hughes, Joe "Guitar," 89–90, 133

"I Gotcha," 96

"I've Been Out There," 110, 123, 125–26

Jackson, Joe, 85

Jackson, Michael, 85

Jackson 5, The, 85

Jacquet, Illinois, 18, 22, 41, 84

James, Elmore, 161

James, Etta, 72, 77–78, 125, 155

James, Joe, 143

Jazz Crusaders, The, 22

John, Little Willie, 52, 62, 64, 65, 67, 70, 82, 125

Johnson, Conrad, 122

Johnson, Evelyn, 30

Johnson, Lonnie, 25

Johnson, Vonell, 143

Jones Hall, 159

Jordan, Louis, 18, 22, 27, 33, 85, 89

Joseph, Walter, 122, 124

"Jump Start," 146–48

Kashmere Stage Band, 102

Kazanoff, Kaz, 122, 131

"Keep a Knockin'," 52

Kennedy, President, 71

Kiel Auditorium, 72, 78

King (saxophone), 17, 36
King, B.B., 20, 30, 62, 72, 88–89, 106, 137
King, Martin Luther (Jr), 70, 93
"Knock on Wood," 138

LaBelle, Patti, 77
Lambert, Lloyd, 122
Lanier, Larry, 2
Laws, Hubert, 22
Leachman, Cloris, 118
Lee, David, 122, 124
Lee, Peggy, 64
Lewis, Earlie Huntsberry, 134–35
Lewis, Elgin, 98
Lewis, Howard, 85
Lewis, Robert, 128, 149
Lewis, Smiley, 26
Life and Times of Little Richard: The Authorised Biography, 40, 59
Lightfoot, Jerry, 106–07
Little Richard & The Crown Jewels, 89
Long Beach Blues Festival, 140, 158
"Long Tall Sally," 6, 48
Lynn, Trudy 159, 161

Mansfield, Jayne, 46
Mayes, Pete, 84
McDaniel's Lounge; 90
McGonigel's Mucky Duck, 116
McGruder, George, 19
McNeely, Big Jay, 112
Medwick, Joe, 34, 90, 108, 110, 123, 125–26, 130–31
Meters, The, 131
"Midnight Hour," 36
Mighty Mighty Clouds of Joy, The, 36
Mills, Nelson III, 146–47, 155, 157
Milton, Roy, 28
Moore, Gil, 39
Moore, Henry, 90
"Mr. Rock 'n Roll," 48
Muldaur, Maria, 114
"Mustang Sally," 138

Nash, Henry, 55, 60, 69
Nelson, Jimmy "T-99," 84, 134
Nelson, Tracy, 90
Neville Brothers, The, 114
"Night Train," 19

Oakman, Joe, 25
"Oh Little Girl," 61
"Okie Dokie Stomp," 37
Owens, Calvin, 20, 84, 106, 147

"Pack Fair and Square," 36
Paramount Theater, 51
Parker, Annise, 158
Parker, Charlie, 27
Parker Music Co., 17
Parker, Sammy, 1
Peacock Studios, 20, 30, 32–33, 40, 61, 110
Perry, Chris, 158
Perry, Johnny, 24, 90, 108, 124
Pharms, Clemet Nell, 115, 139, 163
Platters, The, 46, 155
Porter, George Jr, 131
Powers, Teddy, 85
Pretty Grady Gaines, 90
Price, Walter "The Thunderbird," 32–33, 36

"Rain Drops," 61, 63
Raymond Taylor & The Tempo Toppers, 39
Regal Theater, 51, 78
Restelli, Rick, 155
Richard, Little: and Grady Gaines joining The Upsetters, 1; Chuck Connor recalls meeting Grady, 2; Grady on Richard as a performer, 5; and white artists covering Richard's songs, 6; influenced by Oddis Turner's playing style, 22; on Blues Ramblers break up, 24; Grady matching sax style to Richard's vocals, 28; Grady playing a Selmer saxophone, 36; and Richard with the Tempo Toppers, 39; his

fight with Don Robey, 40; performing at Long Beach Blues Festival, 42; appearance in "The Girl Can't Help It" film, 46; touring in the south, 49; L.C. Gaines recalls Richard's visit to California, 53; and aborted Australian tour, 59; Dee Clark's singing style similar to Richard's, 60; and Richard leaving music business, 81; on Dee Clark recording "Every Night About This Time," 63; and Grady designing stage outfits for Richard, 81; on Grady adapting playing style to particular artists, 86; Paul David Roberts recalls performing with, 111; Roy Gaines on the "Texas Sound," 133; Patrick Harris recalls performing with, 138; Nell Pharms on his appearance in Long Beach, 139; and Greg Gormanous on Richard's performance at Long Beach Blues Festival, 140; and Nelson Mills, III on Grady performing with Richard, 147; Patrick Harris on Richard at Long Beach Blues Festival,158
Richards, Ann, 144
Richards, Wayne, 146, 148, 155, 157
River Café, 105, 116, 117–19
Roberts, Paul David: on meeting Grady, 108; on joining the Texas Upsetters, 111; on Grady and band stage wardrobe, 120; and "Full Gain" album, 123; and "Blues-a-Rama" album, 130; Hammond Scott on Roberts playing on "Blues-a-Rama" album, 131; on visiting Fats Domino's home, 133; on visiting Amsterdam, 136; on band line up for "Jump Start" album, 146; Nelson Mills, III on horn section approach, 147; on Grady's leadership style, 150; and his gig memories, 158
Robertson, O.C. "Bassie," 2
Robey, Don, 30, 32–33, 37, 40, 84, 111
Rock and Roll Hall of Fame, 65, 77, 161–62
Rockefeller's, 112, 158

Roomful of Blues, 112, 114, 117
Royal Theater, 51
Russell, Emil, 70

Sadler, Bill, 105, 116, 118
Sample, Joe, 22
SAR Records, 70, 77
Scott, Hammond, 113–14, 123, 125, 129, 131, 139, 163
Scott, Joe, 32, 34, 36, 141
Scott, Nauman, 113, 115, 130, 137
Selmer (saxophone), 36
Shady's Playhouse, 37
"Shirley Jean," 36
Shorty, Guitar, 114
Shorty's Place, 90–91
Shotwell, Faye, 21, 78, 101
Sierra Grill, 119
Silver Slipper, 90
Simms Twins, The, 74
Slim, Guitar, 124
Smith, Big Robert, 108–09, 123, 128, 129, 130, 146
Smith, Clifton "King Bee," 24
Smith, Wilbur (pseud. Lee Diamond), 1, 2, 55
"Something on Your Mind," 108, 112, 115, 123, 132, 143, 161
"Soothe Me Baby, Soothe Me," 74
Sparks, Melvin, 81
"Stardust," 18
Stax Records, 86, 92
Stevenson, Pee Wee, 106
Stitt, Sonny, 41
"Strokin,'" 109
Sugar Hill Recording Studios, 122, 130
Sullivan, Charles, 60, 62, 70, 85
Supremes, The, 77
Swann, Jimmy, 39

Taylor, Johnnie, 74, 90, 92, 93
Tempo Toppers, The, 1, 39
Tex, Joe, 95–96
Texas Southern University, 22, 101, 146
Texas Upsetters, The: Robert Lewis on

band members, 128; Earlie Huntsberry Lewis on touring Europe, 134; Greg Gormanous on band playing Louisiana festival, 136; on band continuing to perform in the 1990s, 144; Nelson Mills, III on playing with Grady, 147; Robert Lewis on traveling with band, 149; Reginald Yarborough on Grady's management style, 152; Susan Criner on booking the band, 155; and playing show at Jones Hall, 159; Grady on playing before forming band, 112; and origin of name, 113; Bill Sadler on band playing at River Café, 118–119

Third Ward, 84, 94, 109, 118

Thomas, Sonny, 25

Thornton, Big Mama, 40

"Tighten Up," 146

Tipitina's, 130–31, 133, 138, 161

TSU Toronados, The, 146

Turner, Big Joe, 26

Turner, Oddis, 22, 24

Turrentine, Stanley, 27

"Tutti Frutti," 1–2, 6, 40, 80

"Twistin' the Night Away," 70

Universal Attractions, 63, 77, 85

Upsetters, The: and Grady joining the band, 1; on women on the road, 7; on Lester Hill repairing Grady's sax, 37; and Clifford Burks, 41; on The Upsetters lineup, 42; and playing City Auditorium, 43; and "The Girl Can't Help it" film, 46; on touring in the south, 49; and visiting Grady's relatives in California, 52; and sexual exploits, 54; on Little Richard leaving music business, 60; and Milton Hopkins joining the band, 61; on playing with Little Willie John, 65; backing multiple artists on tours, 69; touring with Sam Cooke, 76; on entertaining the audience, 77; on playing revue tours, 78; "World Famous Upsetters," 81; and Grady leaving the road, 89; on Grady continuing to perform around Houston area, 90; John Andrews recalls arrests at a gig, 94; Milton Hopkins on rumors of Grady's drinking problems, 99; and Grady Gaines Jr. playing in band, 102; Bill Sadler on band playing at River Café, 118; and "Blues-a-Rama" album, 130; Susan Criner on booking the band, 156.

Ultrasonic Studios, 131

Uptown Theater, 51

Vaughan, Stevie Ray, 89

Vee-Jay Records, 61, 63

Vincent, Gene, 46, 59

Vivian's Lounge, 90, 94, 95

Walker, Clay, 158

Walker, Joe Louis, 134

Walker, T-Bone, 24, 28, 30, 33, 38, 100, 114

Wallace, R.P. (Roger Paul), 18

Warwick, Dionne, 72

Waskom, Texas, 9–10, 13, 66

Wayne, Henry, 85

Wells, Junior, 157

Wheatley High School, 22

Whispering Pines, 25–26, 28, 32, 37, 38–39

White, Charles, 40, 59

"Whoopin' and Hollerin'," 36

Wiggles, Mr. (Alexander Randolph), 80

Wilburn, Amos, 25

Willis, Chuck, 24, 28, 125

Wilson, Jackie, 72

Wood, Roger, 84

Yarborough, Reginald, 152, 154–55

"You Send Me," 76

"Your Kind of Love," 36

Other Books in the John and Robin Dickson Series in Texas Music

Texas Blues: The Rise of a Contemporary Sound
Alan B. Govenar

The History of Texas Music
Gary Hartman

I'll Be Here in the Morning: The Songwriting Legacy of Townes Van Zandt
Brian T. Atkinson

Everyday Music
Alan B. Govenar

Deep Ellum: The Other Side of Dallas
Alan B. Govenar and Jay F. Brakefield